HENRIK IBSEN

The Wild Duck

Crofts Classics

GENERAL EDITORS

R. C. Bald, *University of Chicago*

Samuel H. Beer, *Harvard University*

William C. DeVane, *Yale University*

HENRIK IBSEN

The Wild Duck

A NEW AMERICAN TRANSLATION BY

Kai Jurgensen

THE UNIVERSITY OF NORTH CAROLINA

AND

Robert Schenkkan

THE UNIVERSITY OF TEXAS

WITH AN INTRODUCTION BY

John Simon

New York

APPLETON-CENTURY-CROFTS
EDUCATIONAL DIVISION
MEREDITH CORPORATION

introduction

"It is hardly possible to criticize The Wild Duck," declared the eighteen-year-old James Joyce in a lecture, "one can only brood upon it as upon a personal woe." That was a daringly advanced view for 1900, but it came to be the accepted one. By 1934, however, Bertolt Brecht was telling an interviewer, "Works by such people as Ibsen and Strindberg remain important historical documents, but they no longer move anybody. A modern spectator can't learn anything from them." That was meant to be a deliberate provocation, but it, too, has come to be more or less accepted—if only by default of dissenting voices.

A young person confronting Ibsen for the first time nowadays may be more than a little unsure about what he is in for. After Shakespeare, Ibsen may well be the most frequently invoked dramatic presence, but whereas everyone more or less knows what he thinks, or is supposed to think, about Shakespeare, about Ibsen one is far less certain. His plays, in this country at least, are not often enough performed, and when they are, are performed poorly. Not much of interest is being written about him, and what notions about him linger in the ambient air have something to do with his being the first modern dramatist, his having ensconced the stage action firmly among the four (or three) walls of the living room, and his having been a "great realist"—a worthy accomplishment but no longer of burning interest.

Such half-truths and commonplaces are of little use, but neither can the problem of Ibsen be resolved by saying that every great literary reputation suffers, after a while, a temporary eclipse, only to be reinstated later as a classic. To begin with, there are too many exceptions to this so-called rule: Chekhov, for example, shows no sign of being relegated to oblivion, and even Strindberg, who was indeed buried, as in Brecht's remark, in the same grave with the Ibsen he hated and was hated by, is beginning to be busily resurrected, while Ibsen is allowed to moulder. Moreover, to become a firmly established classic is no guarantee of anything: it may mean no more than being exhumed and reburied in a massive mausoleum, there to be somewhat more respectfully ignored.

If the neglect of Ibsen cannot be explained simply in terms of generations reacting excessively to one another, it cannot be accounted for even by that somewhat more pertinent generalization that Ibsen has been confused in our minds with the Ibsenites, his various disciples and imitators, and that the sins of the children have been visited upon the father. All one can say for certain is that, for whatever reason, critics and scholars (with some honorable exceptions) have tended to misunderstand or oversimplify him, so that it is no surprise to find a reputable academician summarizing Ibsen's alleged message as "the necessity of clinging to the maximal ideal, however futile." Even if this were substantially true—as, except for one of the major plays, it is not—it would still be crudely condescending: can one sentence ever encapsulate a major artist's mean-
ıgs?

But it is significant that even distinguished fellow-artists
'e been prone not to recognize Ibsen's worth. Thus
'ry and Cocteau once intensely irritated Gide by pro-
ing the lively but mediocre Octave Feuillet far su-
to Ibsen, whom Valéry dismissed as assommant, a
g bore. D'Annunzio rejected Ibsen because of his
' beauty," but Ibsen himself, indirectly, answered
⌐ ᴜₕₐᵣge in a letter to Georg Brandes: "The Latin's aesthetic principles are quite different from ours: he wants absolute formal beauty, while to us conventional ugliness may be beautiful by virtue of its inherent truth." For D. H. Lawrence, Ibsen was, like Strindberg, "a bit wooden . . . a bit skin-erupty." For Yeats, he was "the chosen author of very clever young journalists, who, condemned to their treadmill of abstraction, hated music and style"; in Rosmersholm, Yeats saw "symbolism and a stale odour of split poetry." Max Beerbohm, for whom, as for many critics, Ibsen fell into the ambiguous category of "dramatist of ideas," wrote: "That is the dangerous thing about new ideas: they are old so soon." Ibsen's characters, Max carped, had a way of being mouthpieces for ideas that became, if accepted, truisms; if rejected, "irritating little old paradoxes." But Max at least foresaw that by the end of

our century Ibsen's characters, having gradually grown younger again, would make their creator much admired.

In Austria and Germany, countries friendly to Ibsen's theatre, there was, again, no lack of imperception. That master-critic, Karl Kraus, while esteeming the plays up to Emperor and Galilean, deplored Ibsen's desertion of poetry to become "a rationalist of the miraculous who yet made out of the soberest thing in the world, out of social criticism, a dramatic abracadabra." "We younger ones," Kraus went on to say, "do not grasp much more of the Ibsen of the bourgeois dramas than that he has become the apostle of lady candidates for the schoolteacher's licence." Even Gerhart Hauptmann, much as he had loved and learned from Ibsen, was to note, "Ibsen's dramas are shadow plays." But perhaps the most unfair comment on Ibsen, because it is couched in the ostensible form of judiciously circumscribed praise, occurs in a letter of Henry James's: "Yes, Ibsen is ugly, common, hard, prosaic, bottomlessly bourgeois—and with his distinction so far in, as it were, so behind doors and beyond vestibules, that one is excusable for not pushing one's way to it. And yet of his art he's a master—and I feel in him, to the pitch of almost intolerable boredom, the presence and the insistence of life." But James hastens to add that if genius in the contemporary theatre were "otherwise represented," Ibsen's mastery, "so bare and so lean," wouldn't count for nearly so much.

I have dwelt at such length on these censures and strictures because they sum up compactly the various objections through which we must today fight our way to Ibsen, which we must answer to our full satisfaction before genuine appreciation can begin. It would be a pity indeed not to bring off this rebuttal, for we should then have to forfeit the rewards of a playwright about whom Pirandello, so different an artistic temperament, was to say, "After Shakespeare, without hesitation, I put Ibsen first."

Ibsen, it would seem to emerge from the attacks, is a writer of problem plays concerned with ideas of interest to his particular time; also, he is the purveyor of a slightly rancid symbolism. He is preoccupied with the dreariest bourgeois realities to the point of becoming a bore, yet he is somehow unreal and shadowy. He turns the simplest things into a complicated mystique, but then, again, he is as bare and lean and literal as (*if* I understand Lawrence's "skin-erupty" correctly) a pimply youth. These rather contradictory charges appear to be referring to at least two different authors, but that, in itself, does not invalidate them. For Ibsen wrote at least three different kinds of drama, as he himself indicated when he made his allegorically autobiographical Master Builder Solness tell about the three kinds of buildings he erected in three phases of his life. In accord with Solness's description of his structures (churches, plain dwellings, and a combination of the two), it has become customary to view Ibsen's career as a kind of Hegelian process: the early romantic plays and metaphysical verse dramas (thesis); the sober, socially concerned plays, prosaic and dialectical, of the middle period (antithesis); and, lastly, works introducing symbolic and visionary elements into realistic situations and dialogue (synthesis). Although there is obvious justification for this schematization of Ibsen's development, there are reasons for not swallowing it whole. For one thing, the division is not that rigid: one can find individual scenes within almost any play of Ibsen's that hark backward or look forward. For another, the danger of this view is the implication that the last phase, because it blends the principal strains of the two preceding ones, must needs surpass them in quality. Now, though I would agree that one of these last plays, The Master Builder, is probably Ibsen's best, that does not mean that Little Eyolf is better than Peer Gynt, or that John Gabriel Borkman is to be preferred to Ghosts.

Once we recognize, however, the variety within Ibsen's work, we realize that none of the cited charges can bear on more than one aspect of it, and that sweeping condemnations are likely to mean insufficient acquaintance with the writings as a whole. But the objections might still be valid at least as far as some part or aspect of Ibsen's creation is concerned, and so need to be examined one by one. Let us begin with the charge of excessive bourgeois realism, and its apparent complement, that of mistily vague symbolism, as they might apply to The Wild Duck.

That Ibsen's sympathies were not with the bourgeoisie —or, for that matter, with the lower classes—he was at no pains to hide. It was in a speech to, of all people, the workingmen of Trodhjem, that Ibsen declared "real liberty" to be "beyond the power of the present democracy" to achieve. "An element of aristocracy," he continued, "must enter into our national life, our administration, our representative bodies, and our press." "Of course," he added, "I am thinking of an aristocracy of character, of mind, and will." The fact remains that an aristocracy (or nobility), even if of mind rather than birth, is not a bourgeois concept, and Ibsen made it plain in all his plays that he had little sympathy with the bourgeois way of life. True, Hjalmar Ekdal is patently bourgeois, not the least so in his spurious aspirations to be something else, but Hjalmar is very clearly an anti-hero. Ibsen may write his publisher that "long daily association with the characters of this play has endeared them to me, despite their manifold failings," but that shows only that, like any true artist, he gets inside his creations, not that he shares their values.

If we look for Ibsen's sympathies in the play, they lie chiefly with Hedvig and Dr. Relling, and perhaps, to some extent, also with Gina. But Gina is definitely plebeian, whereas Relling, whatever his origins and in spite of his calling, has become a bohemian. As for Hedvig, in her capacity for love and her love of beauty, she is patently a member of Ibsen's nobility, as her Viking name further suggests.

So much for the "bourgeois." But what about the realism? I should think that, in itself, realism is hardly a pejorative label. It has not harmed Balzac or Dickens, Tolstoy or Thomas Mann. The question is merely whether the naturalistic detail is redeemed by sufficient resonance, whether it does not exhaust itself—and us—in simple enumeration. Here it is relevant to examine Ibsen's language, and it is only fitting to pick the very passage Karl Kraus contemned: Hedvig has just said of the wild duck that "nobody knows who she is, and nobody knows where she comes from even."

GREGERS: And she's been down in the depths of the sea.
HEDVIG (looks quickly at him, suppresses a smile and asks): Why do you say "depths of the sea"?
GREGERS: What else should I say?
HEDVIG: You could have said "the sea bed" or "the bottom of the sea."

> GREGERS: Can't I just as well say "the depths of the sea"?
>
> HEDVIG: Yes, but it sounds so strange to me when someone else says "the depths of the sea."

It will be noticed immediately that there is something poetic, or, at the very least, hypnotic in the way Ibsen uses repetition here. It becomes more than a mere incantatory refrain, more even than the evocation of a trance-like state in which every reiteration transports the speakers farther down toward the depths of the sea. It conveys, above all, Hedvig's rapt astonishment at the fact that someone else uses the romantic, idealistic vocabulary of her fairy-tale vision; it explains why and how Gregers gains his baleful ascendancy over the girl; and, finally, it establishes for us the tragicomic kinship between the deleteriously foolish idealism of the adult and the touching, perilous idealism of the child.

Throughout this play, Ibsen manages to use his "realistic" dialogue very much in the manner of a poet, which he had been and never quite ceased to be, whatever he might say, and however much he might give up writing plays in verse. It is with a poet's care that Ibsen, in the Norwegian, attuned his ear to each character's particular diction; as he warned a translator, "each person in the play has his own special, individual way of speaking, by means of which his degree of education or learning can be noted." But the control of language goes much farther. When, for instance, Hjalmar, overdramatizing things in his customary fashion, refers to Hedvig as an intruder, and the unhappy girl, trembling, asks barely audibly, "Is that me?" [1] the use of these three tiny, incredulous, anguished monosyllables is infinitely more moving and poetic than any longer, more deliberately pathetic, utterance could be. Again, Hjalmar's grandiloquent periphrases and euphuisms —like the references to his father as "that poor old silver-haired man," when, in fact, he is bald and wears a dirty reddish wig—have a way of achieving heights of the anti-poetic accessible only to the true poet. Moreover, as we shall see later, Ibsen is a virtuoso of imagery, a talent

---

[1] The translators have very correctly translated the three Norwegian monosyllables, "Er det mig?" with the tersest English equivalent.

hardly consistent with prosaism. For the moment, consider only Hjalmar's histrionic description of Hedvig to Gregers: "She's as happy and carefree as a little bird—flying straight into a life of endless night." He is, of course, referring to her approaching loss of sight, but the phrase-making clearly suggests how insensitive Hjalmar is to the true meaning of his daughter's impending blindness. However, the trashy sentimentality of "little bird" and "a life of endless night" contains a harrowing, prophetic truth undreamt of by the speaker: Hedvig ends up taking the little bird's place as sacrificial victim, and she does fly straight—not into a life of endless night, but, more dreadfully, the endless night of death.

This brings us to the matter of Ibsen's symbolism, and the shadowy or "split" poetry of which he has likewise been accused. As in the case of realism, there is nothing wrong with symbolism per se, unless, as with Maeterlinck and certain fin-de-siècle writers, it ceases to be grounded in reality, so that the symbols, having no longer any recognizable life in them, become shadows, shadows not even cast by human bodies. But consider now the central symbol of the wild duck. She is, first, a very real bird, serving as a mirror for the various characters' attitudes toward life: old Ekdal, for example, dodderingly relives his past as a great hunter in her; Hjalmar relishes her as "the aristocrat of the attic" endowing him with status. To Gregers, she is that illusion he is determined to uproot; to Gina, a harmless whim in which a wise woman indulges her family; to Hedvig, the promise of all that beauty of which her impoverished childhood is deprived. As such, the duck is entirely believable and a thoroughly functional dramatic device.

But the duck is also a complex and multilaterally operative symbol. She lives, wounded yet almost normal, in a make-believe natural habitat, an attic that postures as sea and woods. She survives well enough, and yet she does not belong among these tame, insipid pigeons and hens. In this sense, she stands for beings like Hjalmar and Hedvig, who live in imaginary worlds: Hjalmar in that of his own genius, Hedvig in that of her egotistical father's love, a love that she has to invent for herself. Hjalmar is wounded by his weakness, his megalomania; Hedvig by her dimming eyesight, the drabness of her present and future, the very fragility of puberty. Yet the illusion of forest, sky, sea—of greatness, freedom, beauty—keeps them going. Would it have been better for the duck to die of its wounds in the depths of the sea?

Gradually, the duck absorbs into herself that illusion, or life-lie, that Gregers is out to destroy. Thus Hedvig's last act takes on an intensely symbolic significance. But the act is, first of all, psychologically right and true to life. Hedvig does not go into the attic to immolate herself, as Mary McCarthy and some others extravagantly suppose. A girl in the difficult phase of puberty, Hedvig is, besides being intelligent and charming, what the French call une petite exaltée, or, rather, she becomes one, goaded by Gregers's malefic hints and by Hjalmar's rejection of her. Very plainly she exclaims, as she leaves the stage, "The wild duck!"—she will now shoot her dearest possession to regain her father's love. Suicide is not at all on her mind, nor any grand, symbolic self-identification with the duck. But confronted with the deed (note how much time elapses before the shot is heard), she cannot do it. Rather than kill the beloved creature, and profoundly miserable as she already is, she prefers to kill herself. It is at this point only that the symbolism takes over: man cannot slay the illusion, the life-lie, he lives by—if he tries to, he kills himself.

This does not yet exhaust the wild duck's symbolic value. She is also an emissary of the mystery that surrounds life; as Hedvig put it, one knows neither who the duck is, nor whence she comes. In that sense, her very presence, so incongruous and, somehow, provocative in that attic, embodies the incursion of the natural world, of forces beyond man's control or ken, into his everyday life. When the duck is mentioned, the persons of the play seem to become more passionately alive, the dialogue quickens and takes on overtones not entirely canny. And for this reason, too, it is fitting that Hedvig should be unable to shoot and extinguish a being that represents something bigger than man and unconquerable by him.

When one assesses how much this symbol concentrates, deepens, and sums up the action and meaning of the play, and with what insight, assurance, and naturalness Ibsen handles it, one is amazed that anyone should have questioned Ibsen's right to his symbolism. Thus it is incompre-

hensible how Brian W. Downs, after making some cogent
remarks about the duck, can still consider her a "detach-
able" part of the play, "a grace note," merely because Ibsen did not have her in his first draft and because the plot
does not absolutely require her presence. Surely the fact
that a drama would have validity even were it less power-
ful, or the circumstance that the poet-playwright found his
perfect expression only after some groping, cannot be sufficient cause for doubting the germaneness of a triumph of
the imagination.

What, next, of Beerbohm's charge, that Ibsen is essen-
tially a playwright of new ideas, of problem plays with
topical interest, in short, a polemist? It is true that polemic, unlike realism or symbolism, is likely to be artistically
limiting. As Max pointed out, specific social issues cease
to matter. One or two lesser plays of Ibsen's, The League
of Youth, for example, do fall into the problem-play category, and can, indeed, be dismissed today. It is true even
that a much better work, An Enemy of the People, has
elements of the problem play about it (though the propa-
gandistic aspects became underlined only in Arthur Miller's
adaptation—a telling example of the difference between
Ibsen and one of the Ibsenites); it is also true that The
Wild Duck, written in part as an answer to An Enemy of
the People, to show the other side of the coin, might seem
in part polemical. In the earlier play, intransigent, heroic
idealism is shown as the only honorable way of life, however fraught with peril; whereas in The Wild Duck, Ibsen
reveals how impractical, obtuse, and disastrous idealism
can be in the wrong hands, wrongly applied. Even An
Enemy of the People, however, is far from being a mere
tract: for one thing, the polluted water and the unmasking
of the corruption that fosters it function as symbols for
the state of society and Ibsen's dramatic fight for truth; for
another, the issues are so basic, the conflicts so timeless,
the characters so gripping, that the play has the same kind
of eternal artistic validity that, say, Coriolanus has.

But as for The Wild Duck, if it has any polemical
character, the polemic is strictly against Ibsen himself: in
Dr. Stockmann, he had shown himself in a highly idealized
light; in Gregers Werle, he caricatures himself relentlessly.
Beyond that, in what possible sense can The Wild Duck
be considered time-bound? The issue is clearly between

those who believe in "the claim of the ideal" and the partisans of "the life-lie," and that battle is not to be localized in space any more than in time. Eric Bentley is very right when he observes in his In Search of Theater that Ibsen "is less interested in 'modern ideas' themselves than in certain ideas that go behind them. In Ibsen one must always look for the idea behind the idea."

And the charge of "lack of beauty," as voiced by d'Annunzio, what of that? What of James's all too willing concession that Ibsen is "ugly, common, hard, prosaic?" The fact is that the mere handling of various kinds of imagery in The Wild Duck should dispel any such notions: poet's images, for Ibsen in his lyrics and verse dramas was very much the poet; and painter's images, for Ibsen was also a not ungifted painter, and might have developed further in that direction had not his wife insisted that he stick to drama.

Take, first of all, the lighting of each act, to which Ibsen urged producers to pay careful attention. In the first act, in Werle's well-appointed study, there are those green-shielded lamps that shed a muted, viridescent light. Northam and other critics have recognized in this a reminder of the forests and their revenge, about which old Ekdal keeps babbling; as well as of the sea-deep from which the wild duck was dragged. Certainly this light is also a reminder of the blindness that it settling on Haakon Werle, and that, directly or indirectly, is to infect the Ekdal household. At the Ekdals', the second act is moonlit, to underscore the romantic illusions being nurtured there; the third takes place on a bright morning, in the kind of light equally suited to false cheerfulness and rude awakenings; the fourth, in the growing darkness of descending evening as misery progressively enwraps the family; the fifth, on a grey, snowy, disconsolate day almost inviting disaster. Again, the bipartite division of both sets, with a front room for the facts of life, so to speak, and another in back, for the feasts money can buy or the dreams poverty can feed on, is conceived along splendidly painterly lines. So, too, are such striking individual images as when Gregers complains of the dark in which the Ekdals live, and Gina, with touching innocence, removes the shade from the lamp.

But Ibsen does not excel merely in such visual imagery;

his verbal-intellectual images are no less commanding.
Take the whole series of references to eyes and seeing. We
hear from Werle, Sr., that his wife's eyes had been "befogged," presently we see Werle's guests and wife-to-be
playing blindman's buff, and we have already learned that
Werle is losing his sight. So the unfortunate Gregers seems
to have blindness of one kind or another on both sides of
his family, and in his social class as well. Hjalmar, too, is
a non-seer. As the first act concludes with the symbolic
game of blindman's buff, the second ends with Hjalmar's
dozing off even as he jibbers about his great forthcoming
invention in the field of photography—itself a form of
seeing—but an invention that will never come about. Thus
Gina's words that end the act, "Shh! Don't wake him up,"
take on added, poignant meaning. Gregers's ailment (and
how modern Ibsen is in making Dr. Relling observe that
we are all crazy or sick) is his befogged vision of reality;
Hjalmar's is being asleep and not seeing at all. But to shut
one's eyes to life is less catastrophic than to see distortedly
and distortingly; still, Gregers announces to his father that
he will "open Hjalmar Ekdal's eyes." Marvel of marvels:
the purblind shall lead the sleeper!

The image takes on darker hues. The jealous and out-
raged Hjalmar, characteristically forgetting that his own
daughter is going blind, exults in Werle's approaching
affliction. When he declaims about retribution for what
he calls Werle's blinding of an innocent fellow-creature—
which is his grandiloquent way of referring to his father's
imprisonment (as much the old man's fault as Werle's, by
the way)—Gina is rightly terrified: Hedvig, as Hjalmar
doesn't know and mustn't find out, is the fruit of Gina's
affair with Werle; if there is to be retribution as well as
heredity, what chance has poor Hedvig got? Echoes of the
biblical eye for an eye further contribute to the somber
ludicrousness of Hjalmar's rhetoric. When Hjalmar, later,
in connection with Werle's deed of gift to Hedvig, exclaims, "Now I'm beginning to see!" and, still later, as
unbeknown to him Hedvig is about to shoot herself, re-
iterates, "My eyes have been opened," the eye-image grows
into something enormous and outrageous and not the less
tragic for being absurd. In The Life of the Drama, Eric
Bentley properly insists that "Hjalmar Ekdal is the classi-
cal instance . . . of tragedy intensified, instead of light-

ened, by comedy." How fearfully appropriate this tragi-comic master-image is to a play in which neither of the co-perpetrators comes to see anything in the tragedy: Gregers will go on being the thirteenth at table, and Hjalmar will make pretty speeches at Hedvig's grave.

Ibsen's imagery aptly subserves the bitter irony and jarring comedy that make The Wild Duck one of the finest tragicomedies in all dramatic literature. So Gregers's mishap with the stove is a masterly example of the use of a symbolic incident to epitomize a character with concision and wit. Gregers makes a mess of trying to start a fire (kindle a passion for the ideal) and of putting the damper on the stove (or on his victims' life-giving illusions). To rescue the situation, he throws his dirty water on the stove (projects his own sickness onto other people), and when he has smelled up and flooded everything, he walks out on the debacle, leaving it to the others to clean up after him if they can.

Similarly, the scenes between Hjalmar and his father are exemplary comic revelations of character, which, needless to say, does not mean that they must elicit loud laughter. Yet this is clearly a very long way from "the intolerable boredom" James, whose plays could never hold an audience, attributed to Ibsen. Granted, the ironic comedy of the play is, if not black, mostly charcoal grey, but the harrowing inner laughter it begets is laughter all the same, emotionally and intellectually stimulating. It was the poet-dramatist Hugo von Hofmannsthal who described the characters in Ibsen's plays as living "in unbearable, painful, depressing little yellowish-grey relationships," and nothing could be more yellowish-grey than the manner in which the Ekdals indulge one another's whims and foibles. But the irony is susceptible of heightening to the point of horror, a horror to which the grotesque undertone adds the stridently discordant note that makes us wince even as we would weep. I am thinking of the Hjalmar-Hedvig scenes: the thoughtless cruelty of Hjalmar, bringing a Hedvig starved alike for affection and good food, not the tidbit he promised, but a menu from the rich man's table. Adding insult to injury, he decries the quality of the delicacies he ate, while promising to give the girl a description of exactly how each one tasted. Not only does this episode evoke, with the economy of superior comic insight, the egotistic hypocrisy and heedless hurtfulness of Hjalmar, but it also shows up his supposed kindnesses for the envenomed darts they are. I do not think that the massacre of Lady Macduff and her children or the spectacle of the blinded and abject Oedipus can affect us more painfully than this scene, or that subsequent one in which, after rationalizations about his health, the perfectly well Hjalmar allows the wretched Hedvig with her fading eyesight to toil in poor light at his job of retouching photographs. And then, cruelest of all, his warning: "But don't ruin your eyes! Do you hear me? I'm not going to be responsible."

Yet the most overpowering example of this brutal irony is still to come, the scene in which, while Hedvig is about to shoot herself through the fault and for the sake of Hjalmar, that fool is blaming Relling and Molvik for his having lost his hat, and shouts about how he will not lose his life by going out hatless into the cold. And it is while he is orating about how Hedvig would not give up a rich life with the Werles that the shot with which Hedvig gives up her poor life is heard. Finally, and no less horribly, what hurts Hjalmar most about Hedvig's death is that he will now be unable to tell her how much he loved her. Egocentricity could not be carried to greater heights, and yet Ibsen manages to make his failed artist, inventor, husband, and father —this human being manqué—for all his hideousness, above all a pitiful oaf. The comic incompetence that dogs him through life, as Gregers hounds him with his claim of the ideal, makes the story more gruesome; but it also enables us the better to recognize Hjalmar's kinship with our own unheroic selves and so forgive this hypocrite actor, our fellow, our brother.

Humor is omnipresent in this grim play. It is there in Gregers's deflation of Hjalmar's high-flown sophistry about the courage he showed in choosing life over suicide with the devastating understatement, "Will, that depends on how you look at it." It is there, doubly, in Hjalmar's sublime response to Gina's question whether she should prepare for his departure or his staying on with the Pythian, "Pack—and fix the room," wherein the absurdity of contradiction is heightened by Hjalmar's grand refusal to perform either task himself. And what of the marvelous triple irony in Relling's remark about righteousness being the Norwegian national disease, but that it appears only sporadically; not only is this a joke at the expense of both righteousness and Norway, but also, what kind of an endemic is one that hardly ever occurs? With these samples of Ibsen's humor, let us conclude our debate with his sundry detractors.

There remains the sovereign question: why has The Wild Duck—original yet universal, poetic yet witty, savage yet humane, symbolic yet earthy—survived as an acknowledged, but not a beloved and popular, masterpiece? Does it, perhaps, lack something, after all? Two things, to be sure, are patently missing: a love interest and a hero. It would seem that the public can forgive one or the other of these omissions, but not both.

That there is no love interest in the play is plain enough; indeed, what may be the cause of the worthy Relling's alcoholism is the loss of Mrs. Sörby's love, but was ever lover's disappointment more laconically expressed—in just one line! And is there truly no hero? There is none: Gina and Hedvig, though good people, are too passive; Relling, though he is the nearest thing to a hero, is kept out of sight all too much, perhaps for that very reason. In the new drama of which Ibsen is the fountainhead, "there are no villains and no heroes," as Bernard Shaw, who was so often wrong about Ibsen, rightly remarked. We can be equally sorry for Gregers and Hjalmar, and we can also despise them equally. Rather than heroes or villains, they are awfully clever dogs or wounded, submerged ducks; but what they resemble most are the unhappy rabbits in the attic of an old duffer who kills them for his sport.

"In tragic life," wrote George Meredith, "no villain need be! Passions spin the plot"—but passions are precisely what is most lacking in The Wild Duck; at the utmost there is Hjalmar's sickly love for himself, or Gregers's no less sickly fixation on ideals wholly inappropriate to the mediocre bourgeois who could as easily handle a lance or a rapier. But if there are no passions to spin the tragicomic plot, is there not, maybe, something else?

Ibsen, it should be noted, is the dramatist of depth psychology; not for nothing was Freud to use the heroine of Rosmersholm as the most pronounced specimen of a certain kind of neurosis he wished to describe. It has been cogently argued that Ibsen's plays are profoundly autobiographical in the sense of an interior autobiography: "these divers human beings are nothing but the one Ibsenian human being in the various phases of development"; they are "merely stages of the selfsame inner experience," as Hofmannsthal observed. And, in Robert Brustein's words, "Unable to master his contradictions, [Ibsen] dramatizes them in his plays, grateful for a form in which tensions do not have to be resolved." Hjalmar, Gregers, Relling—all of them are but isolations of certain impulses, tendencies, stirrings within the playwright, but a playwright rich enough in inner experience to subsume us all.

Ibsen's drama delves and descends; from the point of view of the untrained eye, it even recedes. No one has described this process better than Rilke, in that splendid passage of The Notebooks of Malte Laurids Brigge which conjures up and salutes Ibsen, and which reads in part:

> You measured the scarcely measurable: a feeling that rose by half a degree, the angle of deflection of a will weighted with hardly anything which you read off from very near by, the slight clouding in a drop of yearning and that wisp of discoloration in an atom of confidence: these you had to track down and preserve, for in such occurrences was life to be found now, our life, which had slipped into us, which had withdrawn inward, so deep that there were barely any surmises left concerning it.
>
> Such as you were, inclined toward pointing up, a timelessly tragic poet, you were obliged to convert with one swoop these capillary processes into the matters. So you proceeded to the unexampled deed of violence which was your work that searched ever more desperately among the visible for the equivalents of the inwardly perceived.

It is in this inward vision and the ability to find external equivalents for it that Ibsen's achievement lies. Dramatists of all times have had to cope with similar problems, but in a world of drab burghership, incrustated with layers upon layers of philistinism, it was hard indeed to find the deep-buried roots of idiosyncratic motivation, and no less hard to present actions and events dramatic enough yet also credibly the outgrowth of those roots. The drama in Ibsen is spun by discrepancies, tensions, and contradictions: the war of conflicting passions has shrunk to a tug-of-war of floundering uncertainties. Juliet Capulet was fourteen years old when she died; so was Hedvig Ekdal.

Both died by their own hands, but how different the causes of their deaths! The clash that results in Hedvig's suicide takes place between two small men, Hjalmar and Gregers, themselves divided against themselves, and never even cognizant of their clash. Gregers is aware of his ugliness and the ugliness of his background, but would combat it not by making himself finer, but, cravenly, by trying to foist incommensurate nobility on another weak vessel. Hjalmar has intimations of his weakness, as when he momentarily admits that his great invention is a figment, but he cannot combat his faults with actions—only with acting, acting the part of the gallant paterfamilias. And it is out of the petty division of these two self-divided creatures that suddenly, for reasons that are almost no reason at all, a young girl loses her life. It is not passions that spin the plot but the tug of discrepancies.

Or we might call it the struggle between illusion and reality, a warfare, however, in which the combatants have switched uniforms. For the real truth of Gregers is unreal among a bourgeoisie unable to live it and in a world unwilling to house it; the illusions of Hjalmar, on the other hand, contemptible as they may be, are viable, and might, with luck, tender genuine survival. Yet when neither illusion nor reality can any longer be made to stand and be recognized, what is left but ignorant armies shadowboxing by night?

Ibsen's perceptions and language function on appropriately submerged levels; "his distinction," in James's words, "is far in," but rightly so. Yet the drama surfaces wherever it justifiably can. It is "in the imaginative use of unimaginative language," as Bentley has it, that Ibsen's great realism lies, or, to quote F. L. Lucas on The Wild Duck, in "blend[ing] so perfectly together reality, irony, pity, and poetry." So far from agreeing with Brecht's contention that Ibsen no longer can teach us anything, I believe that we are only today beginning to get at his true meanings, meanings so manifold and self-renewing that there is no danger of their ever being exhausted.

John Simon
Drama Critic
The Hudson Review

principal dates in the life of Henrik Ibsen

1828 Ibsen born at Skien, about 60 miles SW of Oslo.

1834–36 Father goes bankrupt.

1844 Apprenticed to a pharmacist at Grimstad.

1846 Has illegitimate child by a servant girl several years his senior. He will later pay for the child's support.

1849 *Catiline*, the first play. A number of subsequent ones, all failures or at best of minor importance, will not be listed here.

1850 Tries to get into the University of Christiania (Oslo).

1851 Theatre-poet (dramaturge) at the Bergen Theatre.

1852 Travels to Copenhagen and Dresden to study their theatres.

1856 *The Feast at Solhaug*, a moderate success. Meets Suzannah Thoresen.

1857 Artistic director at the Norwegian Theatre of Christiania.

1858 Marries Suzannah. One son will be born of this union.

1862 Failure of Christiania's Norwegian Theatre.

1863–64 The Prusso-Danish War disgusts Ibsen with his countrymen.

---

[1] In compiling this tabulation, I was greatly helped by that of F. L. Lucas in his *Ibsen and Strindberg*.

1864   Moves abroad and henceforth lives alternately in Italy and Germany.

1866   *Brand*, the printed text rather than the productions, establishes Ibsen as a major Scandinavian writer.

1867   *Peer Gynt* consolidates his reputation in the North.

1877   *Pillars of Society*, Ibsen's first truly international success: it has taken him a long time.

1879   *A Doll's House*. Ibsen tries unsuccessfully to win the vote for women in Rome's Scandinavian Club.

1881   *Ghosts*.

1882   *An Enemy of the People*.

1884   *The Wild Duck*.

1886   *Rosmersholm*.

1888   *The Lady from the Sea*.

1889   The aging Ibsen, on a Tyrolese holiday, meets a young Austrian girl, Emilie Bardach, with whom he has a Platonic flirtation. Emilie is the main model for Hilda Wangel in *The Master Builder*. In his later years, Ibsen has several such encounters with much younger women.

1890   *Hedda Gabler*.

1891   *Ghosts* flops in London; GBS fights the anti-Ibsen forces. In other parts of Europe, Ibsen is a great success. He returns to Norway and settles in Oslo.

1892   *The Master Builder*.

1894   *Little Eyolf*.

1896   *John Gabriel Borkman*.

1898   Ibsen's 70th birthday gives rise to widespread festivities.

1899   *When We Dead Awaken*, aptly subtitled by Ibsen "A Dramatic Epilogue."

1900   Health begins to deteriorate.

1901   Suffers a paralytic stroke and can no longer write. Stubbornly tries to teach himself the alphabet all over again.

1906   Ibsen dies. His alleged last word, in answer to the nurse's optimistic comment to his wife about his condition, was "Tvertimot!" ("On the contrary!") If he did not actually say it with his dying breath, he certainly said it with every living one.

THE WILD DUCK

The People: HAAKON WERLE, *a manufacturer and merchant*
GREGERS WERLE, *his son*
OLD EKDAL, *a former Army officer*
HJALMAR EKDAL, *his son, a photographer*
GINA, *Hjalmar's wife*
HEDVIG, *their daughter, fourteen years old*
BERTHA SÖRBY, *Werle's housekeeper*
RELLING, *a doctor*
MOLVIK, *a tutor*
PETTERSEN, *Werle's servant*
GRAABERG, *Werle's bookkeeper*
JENSEN, *a hired waiter*
A PALE, FAT GENTLEMAN
A THIN-HAIRED GENTLEMAN
A NEAR-SIGHTED GENTLEMAN
SIX OTHER GENTLEMEN
SEVERAL HIRED WAITERS

The Place: *Oslo, Norway*
ACT I—*The home of Mr. Werle*
ACT II-V—*Hjalmar Ekdal's studio*

The Time: *Winter, 1884*

1

Approximate Pronunciations: HAAKON WERLE: *Hoken Verlë*; GREGERS: *Grayghers*; HJALMAR EKDAL: *Yalmar Aykdal*; GINA: *Cheena*; SÖRBY: *Sirbee*; GRAABERG: *Grawberg*; JENSEN: *Yensen*.

THE WILD DUCK

Act One

THE SCENE: (*A comfortable and expensively furnished study in* MR. WERLE's *house. Bookcases and overstuffed furniture; a desk in the middle of the room, covered with papers and account books. The room is lighted softly by several lamps with green shades. In the rear wall, center, is an open double door. Beyond is a large, elegant room, brightly lighted by lamps and candelabra. Downstage in the right wall, a small hidden door leads to the offices. Down left is a hob grate with a coal fire burning. Upstage of the fireplace, a double door leads to the dining room.*)

AT RISE: (WERLE's *butler,* PETTERSEN, *is putting the study in order. He is wearing livery. A hired waiter,* JENSEN, *dressed in black, is assisting him. In the large room beyond, two or three other hired waiters are moving around, setting things straight, and lighting more candles. From the dining room can be heard the sound of laughter and the hum of many voices in conversation. A knife raps against a glass. The sound is followed by silence. A toast is proposed. Then applause, and the hum of conversation is resumed.*)

PETTERSEN (*Lighting a lamp on the mantelpiece and replacing the shade.*) Will you listen to that, Jensen—the old boy's on his feet now, proposening a long-winded toast to Mrs. Sörby.

JENSEN (*Moving an easy chair forward.*) Then it's

3

true, maybe, what people say, that there's something between 'em?

PETTERSEN. Who the hell knows?

JENSEN. I hear he used to be a regular billy goat in his day.

PETTERSEN. Maybe.

JENSEN. And he's giving this spread in honor of his son?

PETTERSEN. Yeh. He came home yesterday.

JENSEN. I never even knew Mr. Werle had a son.

PETTERSEN. Yes sir, he's got a son. But he always hangs out at the Highdale works. He hasn't been to town once in all the years I've been in this house.

A WAITER (*In the doorway to the other room.*) Hey, Pettersen! There's an old fellow here that—

PETTERSEN (*Mumbling.*) Oh, hell—why does anybody have to come here now?

(OLD EKDAL *appears from the right, in the room beyond. He is dressed in a threadbare overcoat with a high collar, wears woolen mittens, and carries a stick and a fur cap in his hand. Under his arm is a brown paper parcel. He wears a dirty, reddish-brown toupee and a small grey moustache.*)

PETTERSEN (*Going toward him.*) My God—what do you want here?

EKDAL (*In the doorway.*) I've got to get into the office, Pettersen.

PETTERSEN. The awfis was closed an hour ago and anyway—

EKDAL. I heard that downstairs, old man. But Graaberg's still in there. Be a nice fellow, Pettersen, and let

me slip in that way. (*Pointing to the hidden door.*)
I've gone through here before.

PETTERSEN. Well, go ahead then. (*Opens the door.*)
But remember, be sure to go out the right way. We've
got company.

EKDAL. I know,—hmm! Thanks Pettersen, old man,
good old friend. Thanks. (*Mutters softly:*) Fathead!

(*He goes into the office;* PETTERSEN *closes the
door after him.*)

JENSEN. Does he work in the awfis, too?

PETTERSEN. Nah, he just does some extra copying
whenever they need it. But, as a matter of fact, he
used to be real class in his day, old Ekdal.

JENSEN. He looked like he mighta been anything.

PETTERSEN. Yessir. Let me tell you: he used to be a
lieutenant.

JENSEN. The hell he was? A lieutenant?

PETTERSEN. I'm telling you. But then he got into the
lumber business, or whatever it was. They say he's
supposed to have played a pretty dirty trick on Mr.
Werle, sometime or other. In those days the two of
them were partners in the Highdale works, you see.
Oh, old Ekdal and I are great friends, yessir. We've
had a half and half together lots a' times down at
Madam Eriksen's.

JENSEN. He doesn't look like he had much to buy
anybody drinks with.

PETTERSEN. Hell's bells, Jensen, can't you figger it's
me that buys the drinks? Seems to me a fella ought to
be a little decent to people who've known better days.

JENSEN. He went on the rocks?

PETTERSEN. No, I guess it was worse than that. He landed in jail.

JENSEN. In jail!

PETTERSEN. Or maybe it was the Pen. (*Listening.*) Sh! They're getting up from the table.

(*The door to the dining room is thrown open by a couple of waiters, offstage.* MRS. SÖRBY *comes in, in conversation with a couple of gentlemen. After a moment, the whole party follows. Among them is* MR. WERLE. HJALMAR EKDAL *and* GREGERS WERLE *come in last.*)

MRS. SÖRBY (*As she passes, to the butler.*) Pettersen, will you have the coffee served in the music room?

PETTERSEN. Very well, Mrs. Sörby.

(*She and the two gentlemen go into the inner room and then out right.* PETTERSEN *and* JENSEN *go out the same way.*)

A PALE, FAT GENTLEMAN (*to a* THIN-HAIRED GENTLEMAN.) Whew—what a dinner—it was a tough job to get through it.

THE THIN-HAIRED GENTLEMAN. With a little goodwill, you can do the impossible in three hours.

THE FAT GENTLEMAN. Yes, but afterwards, afterwards, my dear Sir!

A THIRD GENTLEMAN. I hear the coffee and maraschino are going to be served in the music room.

THE FAT GENTLEMAN. Good! Then maybe Mrs. Sörby will play us a tune.

THE THIN-HAIRED GENTLEMAN (*Softly.*) I hope

Mrs. Sörby doesn't play us "Goodbye Forever" one of these days, my friend.

THE FAT GENTLEMAN. Oh, don't worry! Bertha won't forget her old friends.

(*They laugh and go into the other room.*)

WERLE (*Softly and dejectedly.*) I don't think anybody noticed it, Gregers.

GREGERS (*Looking at him.*) What?

WERLE. Didn't you notice it either?

GREGERS. What was it?

WERLE. There were thirteen of us at the table.

GREGERS. Oh? Were there?

WERLE (*With a glance towards* HJALMAR EKDAL.) We're used to being just twelve. (*To the others.*) After you, gentlemen.

(*He and the others, with the exception of* HJALMAR *and* GREGERS, *go out through the inner room and to the right.*)

HJALMAR (*Who has overheard the conversation.*) You shouldn't have sent me that invitation, Gregers.

GREGERS. What? This party is supposed to be for me. Why shouldn't I ask my best, and only, friend?

HJALMAR. I don't think your father likes it. I never come here at any other time.

GREGERS. That's what I hear. But I had to see you and talk to you. I think I'll be leaving again soon. Yes, for a couple of old school friends like us, we certainly have drifted far apart, Hjalmar. It's sixteen, seventeen years since we saw each other last.

HJALMAR. Has it been that long?

GREGERS. It certainly has. Well, how are you doing? You look well. You're putting on weight, getting almost stout.

HJALMAR. Oh now, you can't really say "stout." But I expect I look a little more of a man than I did then.

GREGERS. Yes, you do; outwardly, you haven't suffered any.

HJALMAR (*In a gloomy tone.*) But inside, Gregers. Let me tell you that's something else again. You know, of course, about all the terrible things that have happened to me and my family since I saw you last.

GREGERS (*Lowering his voice.*) How are things going with your father now?

HJALMAR. Oh, let's not talk about that. Naturally, my poor father is staying with me. He hasn't anyone else in the world to turn to. But it's terribly hard for me to talk about this. I'd much rather you'd tell me how you've been getting along up at the works.

GREGERS. I've enjoyed the solitude—I've had plenty of time to think a lot of things over.—Come here. Let's make ourselves comfortable.

(*He sits in an easy chair by the fireplace and gestures for* HJALMAR *to sit in the one beside him.*)

HJALMAR (*Softly.*) I want to thank you though, Gregers, for inviting me here to your father's home. I can see now that you don't have anything against me any more.

GREGERS (*Surprised.*) Where did you get the idea I had anything against you?

HJALMAR. You did, the first few years, didn't you?

GREGERS. When?

HJALMAR. After that terrible business. It was natural for you to. After all, your father was on the verge of being dragged into that—oh, that rotten mess.

GREGERS. So I was supposed to have something against you? Who told you that?

HJALMAR. I know you did, Gregers. Your own father told me.

GREGERS (*Startled.*) My father! I see. Hmm—was that why you never wrote to me again—not a word?

HJALMAR. Yes.

GREGERS. Not even when you decided to become a photographer?

HJALMAR. Your father said I'd better not write you about anything.

GREGERS (*Looking straight before him.*) Well, well, maybe he was right. But tell me, Hjalmar: are you fairly satisfied with your work now?

HJALMAR (*Sighing slightly.*) Oh yes, I suppose so. I can't complain. Naturally, in the beginning, it seemed a little strange. It was all so new to me. But of course, everything was changed. My father's ruin—the shame and the humiliation—Gregers—

GREGERS (*Shaken.*) Yes, yes, I know. I understand.

HJALMAR. I couldn't think of keeping on with my studies; there wasn't a penny left. Just the opposite, there were debts. Mostly to your father, I think—

GREGERS. Hmm—

HJALMAR. Well, considering everything, I thought it was best—with a kind of wrench, you see—to tear myself completely away from all the old ties and connections. Your father, particularly, advised me to do it. And since he was taking such a helpful interest in me—

GREGERS. My father was?

HJALMAR. Surely you know that. Where was I going to get the money to learn the trade and equip a studio and get started? That's an expensive business, believe me.

GREGERS. And my father paid for all of it?

HJALMAR. Yes, didn't you know? I understood him to say he'd written you about it.

GREGERS. Not a word about his own connection with it. He must have forgotten. We've never exchanged anything but business letters. So it was my father—

HJALMAR. I should say so. He's never wanted anybody to know about it, but that's who it was. And of course he was the one, too, who made it possible for me to get married. Or—perhaps you didn't know that either?

GREGERS. No, I should say I didn't— (*Shakes him by the arm.*) But, my dear friend, I can't tell you how happy this makes me—and how ashamed. Maybe I've been unfair to my father, after all—in some ways, anyway. Because this shows that he does have a heart. It's almost like a kind of conscience—

HJALMAR. Conscience?

GREGERS. Yes, or whatever you want to call it. I can't tell you how happy I am to hear this about him. That's right, you're a married man, Hjalmar! That's further than I'll ever get. Well, I hope you're happy?

HJALMAR. Oh yes. She's as nice, and as good a wife, as a man could want. And she's not entirely without education.

GREGERS (*A little surprised.*) Why, of course not.

HJALMAR. Oh, no. Life gives you a sort of education, you know. Her daily life with me—and there are a couple of intelligent people who come to see us regularly. Believe me, you would never know Gina again.

GREGERS. Gina?

HJALMAR. Yes, Gregers. Don't you remember her name was Gina?

GREGERS. Whose? I haven't the slightest idea—

HJALMAR. Remember? She used to work here.

GREGERS (*Looks at him.*) Are you talking about Gina Hansen—

HJALMAR. Of course—Gina Hansen.

GREGERS.—who ran the house for us the last year my mother was sick?

HJALMAR. Why certainly. But my dear Gregers, I know for a fact your father wrote you I'd gotten married.

GREGERS (*Who has gotten up.*) Yes, he did; but not that— (*Pacing the floor.*) Yes, wait a minute— maybe he did after all—now that I think of it. But my father always writes me such short letters. (*Sits on the arm of his chair.*) Tell me, Hjalmar—this is very interesting—how did you happen to meet Gina —I mean, your wife?

HJALMAR. It was very simple. As you know, Gina didn't stay in this house very long. Everything here was so confused then. Your mother's illness and—— It was too much for Gina; so she gave notice and left. It was the year before your mother died—or maybe it was the same year.

GREGERS. It was the same year. I was up at the factory at the time. But what then?

HJALMAR. Well, Gina went to live with her mother, old Mrs. Hansen. An awfully nice, hard-working woman. She ran a little boardinghouse. She had a room for rent, too—a very pleasant, comfortable room.

GREGERS. And you were lucky enough to get it, I suppose.

HJALMAR. Well, yes. Actually, it was your father who put me on to it. And it was there—you see—it was there that I really got to know Gina.

GREGERS. And the next thing you knew you were engaged?

HJALMAR. Yes. It's so easy for young people to fall in love—; hmm—

GREGERS (*Rises and drifts about for a minute.*) Tell me,—after you'd gotten engaged—was that when my father—that you—I mean, was that when you decided to take up photography?

HJALMAR. Exactly. I wanted to get started and set up a home—the sooner, the better. And your father and I both thought that this photography business was the easiest way. And Gina thought so, too. And then there was another reason: it turned out, luckily, that Gina knew something about retouching.

GREGERS. What a lucky coincidence.

HJALMAR (*Rises, pleased.*) Yes, wasn't it? Wasn't it a wonderful coincidence?

GREGERS. There's no getting around that. My father seems to have been a regular guardian angel for you.

HJALMAR (*Moved.*) He didn't fail the son of his old friend when hard times came. Because he *has* a heart, you see.

MRS. SÖRBY (*Coming in; arm in arm with* WERLE.) No nonsense now, Haakon. You mustn't stay in there any longer staring at the candles. It isn't good for you.

WERLE (*Lets go of her arm, and passes his hand over his eyes.*) I guess you're right at that.

(PETTERSEN *and* JENSEN *pass trays of punch around.*)

MRS. SÖRBY (*To the guests in the other room.*) All right, gentlemen. If anyone wants a glass of punch he'll have to make an effort and come and get it.

THE FAT GENTLEMAN (*Approaching* MRS. SÖRBY.) For heaven's sake, have you really taken away our sacred right to a smoke?

MRS. SÖRBY. Yes. It's forbidden here in Mr. Werle's sanctum, Sir.

THE THIN-HAIRED GENTLEMAN. When did you introduce the amendments to the smoking law, Mrs. Sörby?

MRS. SÖRBY. Since the last dinner, Sir, when certain persons here permitted themselves to overstep the mark.

THE THIN-HAIRED GENTLEMAN. And it's not permissible to overstep the mark even a little bit, Bertha? Not under any circumstances?

MRS. SÖRBY. Not under any circumstances, Mr. Balle.

(*Most of the guests have gathered in the study. The* WAITERS *pass glasses of punch around.*)

WERLE (*to* HJALMAR, *who is standing by a table.*) What are you so engrossed in, Ekdal?

HJALMAR. Just an album, Mr. Werle.

THE THIN-HAIRED GENTLEMAN (*Who is drifting about.*) Ah, photographs! Yes, I guess that's right in your line.

THE FAT GENTLEMAN (*In an easy chair.*) You didn't by any chance bring any of your own?

HJALMAR. No, I didn't.

THE FAT GENTLEMAN. You should have. It's good for the digestion to sit and look at pictures.

THE THIN-HAIRED GENTLEMAN. And it always adds a little to the entertainment, too.

THE NEAR-SIGHTED GENTLEMAN. And all contributions are gratefully received.

MRS. SÖRBY. The gentlemen mean that if you're invited to dinner, you have to work for it, Mr. Ekdal.

THE FAT GENTLEMAN. After a good meal, that's a pleasure.

THE THIN-HAIRED GENTLEMAN. After all, when it's a matter of the fight for survival—

MRS. SÖRBY. That's the truth!

(*They continue, laughing and joking.*)

GREGERS (*Softly.*) Get into the conversation, Hjalmar.

HJALMAR (*Writhing.*) What'll I talk about?

THE FAT GENTLEMAN. Mr. Werle, don't you think that Tokay can be considered a wine that's comparatively harmless?

WERLE (*By the fireplace.*) I'm not afraid to guarantee the Tokay you had today. It's one of the very finest vintages. Well, of course, you know that, too.

THE FAT GENTLEMAN. Yes, it had a remarkably delicate bouquet.

HJALMAR (*Uncertainly.*) Is there any difference between the—vintages?

THE FAT GENTLEMAN (*Laughing.*) That's a good one!

WERLE (*Smiles.*) It really doesn't pay to put a noble wine in front of you.

THE THIN-HAIRED GENTLEMAN. It's the same way with Tokay as with photography, Mr. Ekdal. It takes plenty of sunshine. Right?

HJALMAR. Yes, I guess the light helps, all right.

MRS. SÖRBY. That's just the way it is with the gentlemen. They're badly in need of sunshine, too—royal sunshine.

THE THIN-HAIRED GENTLEMAN. Ouch! What a worn-out sarcasm!

THE NEAR-SIGHTED GENTLEMAN. The lady is being heard from—

THE FAT GENTLEMAN. —And at our expense. (*He holds up a reproving finger.*) Bertha, Bertha!

MRS. SÖRBY. But it's a fact all the same; there's a lot of difference between vintages. The old ones are best.

THE NEAR-SIGHTED GENTLEMAN. Do I fall into that category?

MRS. SÖRBY. Oh, far from it.

THE THIN-HAIRED GENTLEMAN. So much for you! How about me, my sweet Mrs. Sörby?

THE FAT GENTLEMAN. Yes, and me? What vintage do we belong to?

MRS. SÖRBY. Why, one of the sweet vintages, gentlemen.

(*She sips a glass of punch. The* GENTLEMEN *laugh and joke with her.*)

WERLE. Mrs. Sörby can always find a way out—when she wants to. Drink them down, gentlemen! Pettersen, take care of—! Gregers, suppose we have one together? (*Gregers does not move.*) Won't you join us, Ekdal? I didn't have an opportunity to toast you at the table.

(GRAABERG, *the Bookkeeper, looks in through the hidden door.*)

GRAABERG. Excuse me, Mr. Werle, but I can't get out.

WERLE. Well! Did you get yourself locked in again?

GRAABERG. Yes, and Flakstad has gone off with the keys.

WERLE. You'd better come through here then.

GRAABERG. But there's somebody else—

WERLE. Well, come on, come on, both of you. Don't be embarrassed.

(GRAABERG *and* OLD EKDAL *come out of the office.*)

WERLE (*Involuntarily.*) Agh!

(*The laughter and conversation die out among the guests.* HJALMAR, *startled at the sight of his father, puts his glass down, and turns toward the fireplace.*)

EKDAL (*Does not raise his eyes, but makes little short bows to both sides, as he goes, mumbling.*) Beg pardon. Coming the wrong way. Door's locked. Door's locked. Beg pardon.

(*He and* GRAABERG *go out right, through the inner room.*)

WERLE (*Between his teeth.*) That damn fool, Graaberg!

GREGERS (*Staring open-mouthed, to* HJALMAR.) Why, that couldn't have been—!

THE FAT GENTLEMAN. What's this? Who was it?

GREGERS. Oh, nobody. Just the bookkeeper and somebody else.

THE NEAR-SIGHTED GENTLEMAN (*To* HJALMAR.) Did you know that man?

HJALMAR. I don't know—I didn't notice—

THE FAT GENTLEMAN. What the devil is wrong?

(*He joins some others. They talk together softly.*)

MRS. SÖRBY (*Whispers to Pettersen.*) Give him something out there—something good.

PETTERSEN (*Nods.*) I'll take care of it.

(*He goes out.*)

GREGERS (*Shaken; to* HJALMAR, *softly.*) So it really was he!

HJALMAR. Yes.

GREGERS. And you could stand there, and deny you knew him!

HJALMAR (*Whispers vehemently.*) But how could I—!

GREGERS. —Acknowledge your own father?

HJALMAR (*Painfully.*) Oh, if you were in my place—

(*The conversation among the guests which has been carried on in low tones, now changes to forced gaiety.*)

THE THIN-HAIRED GENTLEMAN (*Approaching* HJALMAR *and* GREGERS *in friendly fashion.*) Aha! Reviving memories of your old college days? Hah? Don't you smoke, Mr. Ekdal? Let me give you a light. Ah, that's right, we're not supposed to—

HJALMAR. Thank you, I don't want—

THE FAT GENTLEMAN. Haven't you got a clever little poem to recite for us, Mr. Ekdal? You used to be so good at it.

HJALMAR. I'm sorry, I can't remember anything.

THE FAT GENTLEMAN. That's too bad. Well, then what can we think of, Balle?

(*Both* GENTLEMEN *cross the room and enter the one beyond.*)

HJALMAR (*Gloomily.*) Gregers—I've got to go! When a man has been dealt such a crushing blow by fate—tell your father goodbye for me.

GREGERS. All right. Are you going straight home?

HJALMAR. Yes. Why?

GREGERS. I might drop by later.

HJALMAR. No, you mustn't. Not at my place. My house is a sad place, Gregers; particularly after a brilliant party like this.

MRS. SÖRBY (*Who has approached; softly.*) Are you leaving, Mr. Ekdal?

HJALMAR. Yes.

MRS. SÖRBY. Say hello to Gina for me.

HJALMAR. Thank you.

MRS. SÖRBY. And tell her I'm going to come see her one of these days.

HJALMAR. I will, thank you. (*To* GREGERS.) Stay here; I want to slip out quietly.

(*He drifts across the stage, then into the other
room, and out right.*)

MRS. SÖRBY (*Softly, to* PETTERSEN, *who has returned.*) Well, did the old fellow get something to
take with him?

PETTERSEN. Yes, ma'm; I slipped him a bottle of
cognac.

MRS. SÖRBY. You ought to have been able to think
of something better than that.

PETTERSEN. No ma'm, Mrs. Sörby. There isn't anything he likes better than cognac.

·THE FAT GENTLEMAN (*Appearing in the doorway
with some sheet music.*) Shall we play something together, Mrs. Sörby?

MRS SÖRBY. All right, let's do that.

GUESTS. Good, good! Hear, hear!

(*She and all the company go through the inner
door and out right.* GREGERS *stays by the fireplace.*
WERLE *looks for something on the desk and ap-
parently wishes that* GREGERS *would go. Since*
GREGERS *doesn't move,* WERLE *starts to leave.*)

GREGERS. Father, wait please.

WERLE (*Stopping.*) What is it?

GREGERS. I'd like to talk to you for a minute.

WERLE. Can't it wait till we're alone?

GREGERS. No, it can't. Maybe we're not going to be
alone.

WERLE (*Coming closer.*) What do you mean by
that?

(*During the following scene, piano music is heard
from the distant music room.*)

GREGERS. Why have you let that family get in such a rotten state?

WERLE. You're talking about the Ekdals, I suppose.

GREGERS. Yes. That's who I mean, the Ekdals. After all, Lt. Ekdal was once very close to you.

WERLE. Too close, I'm afraid. I've paid for it for years. He's the one I have to thank for the stain on my good name and reputation.

GREGERS (*Softly.*) Was he really the only one to blame?

WERLE. Who else? What do you mean?

GREGERS. You and he were partners in that big lumber deal—

WERLE. But wasn't it Ekdal who drew up the map of the sections—that fraudulent map? He was the one who did all that illegal cutting on Government property. He was responsible for the whole project up there. I had no idea what he was doing.

GREGERS. I'm afraid Lt. Ekdal didn't know himself what he was doing.

WERLE. Maybe so. But the fact remains that he was found guilty and I was acquitted.

GREGERS. Yes, I know there was no proof against you.

WERLE. An acquittal is an acquittal. Why bring that business up again? It's given me grey hair before my time. Is that the sort of thing you've been brooding about up there all these years? I can assure you, Gregers, here in town it was forgotten a long time ago—as far as I am concerned.

GREGERS. But what about the poor Ekdals?

WERLE. What do you think I could have done for them? When Ekdal was released he was a broken man, completely beyond help. There are people in this world who sink to the bottom after they have been peppered just once, when they just have a couple of bird shot in them, and never come up again. Believe me, Gregers, I've gone as far as I could without actually laying myself open, and giving rise to suspicion and gossip—

GREGERS. Suspicion? Oh, yes, I see.

WERLE. I've given Ekdal copying to do for the office, and I pay him a lot more than his work is worth—

GREGERS (*Without looking at him.*) I don't doubt that.

WERLE. Are you laughing? You think I'm lying? Naturally, there's nothing about it in my books. I never enter expenses like that.

GREGERS (*Smiles coldly.*) No, I suppose there are certain expenses it's better not to enter.

WERLE (*Taken aback.*) What do you mean by that?

GREGERS (*Gathering his courage.*) Did you enter in your books how much it cost you to have Hjalmar Ekdal learn the photography business?

WERLE. I? What do you mean "enter in my books?"

GREGERS. I've found out that you paid for it. And I found out, too, that it was you who helped him with such generosity to get established.

WERLE. And you still say I haven't done anything for the Ekdals! That family has cost me plenty, I tell you.

GREGERS. Have you carried any of those items in your books?

WERLE. Why do you want to know that?

GREGERS. I have my reasons. Tell me, in those days

when you took such a warm interest in the son of
your old friend—wasn't that just when he was about
to be married?

WERLE. Well—dammit—after so many years—how
can I—

GREGERS. You wrote me a letter then—a business letter, of course—and in a P.S. you said—very
laconically—that Hjalmar Ekdal had married a Miss
Hansen.

WERLE. Well, that was perfectly right. That was
her name.

GREGERS. But you didn't mention that this Miss
Hansen was Gina Hansen—our former housekeeper.

WERLE (*With a forced laugh of contempt.*) No, I
didn't think you were particularly interested in our
former housekeeper.

GREGERS. I wasn't. But— (*Lowering his voice.*) I
guess there was somebody else in this house who was
particularly interested.

WERLE. What are you talking about? (*Flaring up.*)
You're not by any chance aiming at me, I hope!

GREGERS (*Softly but firmly.*) Yes, I am.

WERLE. How dare you! Do you have the nerve to—
How does he—that ungrateful—that photographer—
how does he dare make such an insinuation?

GREGERS. Hjalmar hasn't said a word about it. I
don't think he has even the slightest suspicion.

WERLE. Then where did you get the idea? Who's
said anything like that?

GREGERS. My mother—poor thing. The last time I
saw her.

WERLE. Your mother! Ah, wouldn't you know it!
You and she—you always stuck together. She was the
one who turned you against me, right from the start.

GREGERS. No. It was what she had to suffer from you. Until she gave up and was so pitifully destroyed.

WERLE. She didn't have to suffer anything. Not any more than most people, anyway. But you can't get anywhere with sickly, hysterical weaklings—I ought to know. And you go around nourishing a suspicion like that—grubbing around in all sorts of old rumors and slanders against your own father! Now listen here, Gregers, I certainly think that at your age you could find something better to do.

GREGERS. Yes, it's high time.

WERLE. Maybe you'd be easier in your mind than you seem to be now. What's it going to get you, staying up at the factory, year after year, slaving away like an ordinary clerk, and not taking a cent above the ordinary pay? It's absolutely asinine.

GREGERS. Yes, if I were just sure of that.

WERLE. I know what it is. I understand you. You want to be independent. You don't want to owe me anything. Well, here's your chance to become independent, your own boss, in everything—

GREGERS. Oh? How's that going to—

WERLE. When I wrote you that I wanted you to come to town right away—hmm—

GREGERS. Yes, exactly what is it you want? I've been waiting all day to find out.

WERLE. I want to offer you a membership in the firm.

GREGERS. Me? In your firm? As a partner?

WERLE. Yes. We wouldn't need to be together all the time because of that. You could take over the business here in town, and I'd move up to the factory.

GREGERS. You would?

WERLE. I can't do as much work as I used to. I'm

going to have to go easy on my eyes, Gregers. They've started to get a little weak.

GREGERS. They always were.

WERLE. Not as bad as they are now. And anyway, it might be a good idea, because of certain circumstances, for me to live up there. For a while at least.

GREGERS. I wouldn't have expected that.

WERLE. Listen, Gregers, there are a lot of things that stand between us; but, after all, we're still father and son. I should think we ought to be able to come to some kind of an understanding.

GREGERS. On the surface, you mean?

WERLE. Well, that would be something, at least. Think it over. Don't you think we could? Eh?

GREGERS (*Looking at him coldly.*) There's something behind this.

WERLE. What do you mean?

GREGERS. There must be something you need me for.

WERLE. In a relationship as close as ours, one always needs the other, I suppose.

GREGERS. That's what they say.

WERLE. I'd like to have you at home for a while. I'm a lonely man, Gregers. I've always been lonely— all my life; but most of all now, when I'm beginning to feel my age. I need to have somebody around—

GREGERS. You've got Mrs. Sörby.

WERLE. Yes, I have. And she's become almost indispensable to me, you might say. She's lively. She's dependable. She brightens the house up a lot—and I need that very badly.

GREGERS. Well, you have everything just as you want it then.

WERLE. Yes, but I'm afraid it can't last. A situation like that may put a woman in a very difficult position in the eyes of the world. It doesn't do a man any good, either, I might add.

GREGERS. Oh, if a man can give the kind of dinner parties you do, he can get away with a good deal.

WERLE. All right, but about her, Gregers? I'm afraid she won't put up with it much longer. And even if she would—even if, out of loyalty to me, she were to expose herself to gossip and slander, and things like that— Then, do you think, Gregers—you with your overwhelming sense of justice—

GREGERS (*Interrupting.*) Just tell me one thing: are you thinking of marrying her?

WERLE. And if I were? Then what?

GREGERS. That's what I'm asking. Then what?

WERLE. Would you be absolutely against it?

GREGERS. Not at all. Not in the least.

WERLE. Well, I had no way of knowing whether your regard for your mother's memory—

GREGERS. *I'm* not "hysterical."

WERLE. Well, whatever you are or aren't, at any rate you've taken a great weight off my mind. I'm very happy that I can count on your agreement in this matter.

GREGERS (*Looks intently at him.*) Now I see what you want to use me for.

WERLE. Use you for? What kind of an expression is that?

GREGERS. Oh, let's not be finicky in our choice of words—not when it's just between the two of us, anyway. (*With a short laugh.*) I see. So that's why, come hell or high water, I had to make a personal appearance in town. In honor of Mrs. Sörby, we're going to stage a show of family life in this house—a tableau, father and son! That'll be something new.

WERLE. How dare you speak to me in that tone?

GREGERS. When have we had any home life here? Not since I can remember. But now it seems you could use a little. No doubt it will look good when people say that your son came flying home, on the wings of piety, to the nuptials of his aging father. Then what will be left of all the rumors about what the poor dead woman had to suffer? Not a shred. Her son wipes them out at one fell swoop.

WERLE. Gregers—I don't believe there's anyone else in the world you hate as much as you do me.

GREGERS (*Softly.*) I've seen you too close.

WERLE. You've seen me with your mother's eyes. (*He lowers his voice a little.*) But you ought to remember that those eyes were—a little befogged now and then.

GREGERS (*Trembling.*) I know what you're hinting at. But—mother's unfortunate weakness—whose fault was it? Yours, and all these! The last of them was this female who was wished off on Hjalmar Ekdal when you no longer— Agh!

WERLE (*Shrugs his shoulders.*) Word for word, as if your mother were saying it!

GREGERS (*Paying no attention.*) And there he is, with his great, childlike mind—innocent—right in the midst of this mockery—living with a woman like that, without knowing that what he calls his home is built on a lie! (*Coming a step closer.*) When I look back over your life, it's like looking at a battlefield, with mangled lives lying all along the roads.

WERLE. I'm afraid we are too far apart.

GREGERS (*Bows coldly.*) That's right. So I'm going to get out—

WERLE. You're going? You're leaving the house?

GREGERS. Yes. I've finally found something to live for.

WERLE. What?

GREGERS. You'd only laugh, if I told you.

WERLE. It isn't that easy for a lonely man to laugh, Gregers.

GREGERS (*Pointing towards the inner room.*) Look, father—the gentlemen are playing blindman's buff with Mrs. Sörby. Good night and good luck.

(*He goes out through the inner room and to the right. The laughter and gaiety of the party become audible, and the guests appear in the other room.*)

WERLE (*Muttering contemptuously after* GREGERS.) Ha! Poor devil—and he says he isn't hysterical!

Act Two

THE SCENE: HJALMAR EKDAL's *studio, a large room obviously right under the roof. At right, a great slanting skylight, half covered by blue curtains. In the corner, up right, is the hall door. Downstage, on the same side, is a door leading to the living room. In the left wall there are two doors, and between them an iron stove. In the rear wall is a wide, double sliding door. The studio is simply but comfortably furnished. Between the doors, right, a little out from the wall, is a sofa with some chairs and a table. On the table a lighted lamp, shaded. There is an old easy-chair in the corner by the stove. Distributed here and there around the rooms are various pieces of photographic equipment. Against the rear wall, left of the double doors, is a bookcase containing various books, boxes, and bottles of chemical solutions, also various tools, instruments, and other objects. Photographs, brushes, paper, etc., are scattered about on the table.*

AT RISE: GINA EKDAL *is sitting in a chair by the table, sewing.* HEDVIG *is sitting on the sofa, her hands shading her eyes and her thumbs in her ears, reading a book.*)

GINA (*Glances at her once or twice, hiding her anxiety, then says:*) Hedvig! (HEDVIG *does not hear. More loudly.*) Hedvig!

HEDVIG (*Takes away her hands and looks up.*) Yes, Mother?

GINA. Darling, don't sit there and read any longer.

28

HEDVIG. Oh, Mother, can't I read a little more? Just a little?

GINA. No, no, put that book down now. Your father don't like it; he don't do it himself at night.

HEDVIG (*Closes the book.*) No, Papa doesn't care much about reading.

GINA (*Puts her sewing aside, and takes a pencil and a little notebook from the table.*) Do you remember how much we paid out for butter today?

HEDVIG. One sixty-five.

GINA. That's right. (*Makes a note.*) It's awful how much butter we use in this house. Then there was sausage and cheese—let's see— (*Makes a note.*) and the ham—hmm— (*Adds.*) Well, right there we have—

HEDVIG. Don't forget the beer.

GINA. That's right. (*Makes a note.*) It adds up. But we can't get away from it.

HEDVIG. Well anyway, you and I didn't need anything hot for dinner, since Papa was out.

GINA. No, and that helped. And I did take in eight fifty for the pictures.

HEDVIG. Really! Was it that much?

GINA. Exactly eight fifty.

(*A pause.* GINA *takes up her sewing again.* HEDVIG *takes a piece of paper and a pencil and begins drawing, shading her eyes with her left hand.*)

HEDVIG. Isn't it fun to think of Papa at Mr. Werle's big dinner party?

GINA. You can't really say that he's at Mr. Werle's.

It was the son that asked him. (*After a short pause.*)
You know we don't have anything to do with that
Mr. Werle.

HEDVIG. Oh my, I'm looking forward to Papa's coming home. He promised to ask Mrs. Sörby for something good for me.

GINA. Yes, you can pick up a lot of good things in
that house, believe me.

HEDVIG (*Still drawing.*) I guess I'm a little hungry,
too.

(OLD EKDAL *comes in from the hall. He is carrying a paper parcel under his arm and another in
his pocket.*)

GINA. Hello, Grandpa, you're home late today.

EKDAL. They'd locked the office. I had to wait with
Graaberg. And then I had to go through—hmm.

HEDVIG. Did they give you some more copying,
Grandpa?

EKDAL. This whole package. Just look at it.

GINA. That's fine.

HEDVIG. You've got a package in your pocket, too.

EKDAL. Hah? Nonsense, that isn't anything. (*Puts
his stick in the corner.*) This'll keep me busy for a
long time, Gina. (*He opens one of the double doors
a little way.*) Shhh! (*Peeps into the room for a moment, then closes the door carefully.*) He-he! They're
all asleep, the whole pack of them. And the little
thing's gotten into the basket herself. He-he!

HEDVIG. Are you sure she isn't cold in that basket,
Grandpa?

EKDAL. What an idea! Cold? In all that straw? (*He

goes towards the door up left.) There are matches in there?

GINA. They're on the dresser.

(EKDAL *goes into his room.*)

HEDVIG. It's nice that Grandpa got all that copying to do.

GINA. Yes, poor old fellow; he can make a little pocket money that way.

HEDVIG. And then he won't have time to sit all morning in that awful place of Mrs. Eriksen's.

GINA. That's right, too.

(*A short silence.*)

HEDVIG. Do you think they're still at the table?

GINA. Who knows; might be.

HEDVIG. Imagine! All the wonderful things Papa's getting to eat! He's sure to be in a good mood when he comes home. Don't you think so, Mother?

GINA. Yes, if we could just tell him we'd rented the room.

HEDVIG. Oh, we don't need that tonight.

GINA. Every little bit helps, dear. It's not any use to us now.

HEDVIG. I mean we don't need it tonight because Papa will be in a good mood anyway. It would be better if we kept the room for some other time.

GINA (*Looks at her.*) You like having some good news to tell your father when he comes home at night?

HEDVIG. Yes; it makes things nicer around here somehow.

GINA (*Looks before her, thinking.*) There's some-thin' to that.

(OLD EKDAL *comes in again and is about to go out by the door down left.*)

GINA (*Half-turning in her chair.*) What is it, Grandpa? You want somethin' in the kitchen?
EKDAL. Umh-hum, yes. No, no; stay where you are.

(*He goes out.*)

GINA. I hope he's not messin' around with the fire out there. (*After a moment.*) Hedvig, take a look at what he's doin', will you?

(EKDAL *returns with a little mug full of boiling water.*)

HEDVIG. Are you getting hot water, Grandpa?
EKDAL. Umh-hum, yes. Going to use it for some-thing. Have to write, and the ink's gotten as thick as pudding—hmm.
GINA. You ought to eat your supper first, Grandpa. It's set for you in there.
EKDAL. Never mind about the supper, Gina. Aw-fully busy, I tell you. Don't want anybody to come into my room. Nobody—hmm.

(*He goes into his room;* GINA *and* HEDVIG *look at each other.*)

GINA (*Softly.*) Can you figure out where he got the money?

HEDVIG. I guess Graaberg must have given it to him.

GINA. No chance of that. You know Graaberg always sends the money to me.

HEDVIG. He must have gotten somebody to let him have a bottle on credit somewhere.

GINA. Poor old man! Who'd give him credit?

(HJALMAR EKDAL, *wearing an overcoat and a gray felt hat, comes in at right.*)

GINA (*Throws down her sewing and stands up.*) Why, Hjalmar! Are you back already?

HEDVIG (*Jumping up at the same time.*) Already! That's wonderful, Papa!

HJALMAR (*Puts his hat down.*) Yes, most of them were leaving.

HEDVIG. So early?

HJALMAR. Well, after all, it was a dinner party.

(*He starts to take his overcoat off.*)

GINA. Let me help you.

HEDVIG. Me, too.

(*They help him off with his coat.* GINA *hangs it up on the back wall.*)

HEDVIG. Were there many people, Papa?

HJALMAR. Oh, not many. There were about twelve or fourteen of us at the table.

GINA. And I guess you got to talk to all of them?

HJALMAR. Oh yes, a little. But Gregers particularly; he took up most of my time.

GINA. Is Gregers still as ugly as ever?

HJALMAR. Well, you know, he's not much to look at. Isn't the old man home?

HEDVIG. Yes, Grandpa's in there, writing.

HJALMAR. Did he say anything?

GINA. No, what should he have said?

HJALMAR. Didn't he say anything about— I thought I heard that he'd been with Graaberg. I'll go in and see him for a minute.

GINA. No, no, you'd better not—

HJALMAR. Why not? Did he say he didn't want me in there?

GINA. I don't think he wants nobody in there to-night—

HEDVIG (*Making signs.*) Hmm—hmm!

GINA (*Not noticing.*) —He's been in to get hot water—

HJALMAR. Oh! He's sitting there?

GINA. Yes, I guess so.

HJALMAR. Oh God! My poor, old white-haired father! Well, all right! Let's leave him alone to cheer himself up.

(OLD EKDAL, *wearing a bathrobe and carrying a lighted pipe, comes in from his room.*)

EKDAL. You home? I thought I heard you talking.

HJALMAR. I just got here.

EKDAL. I guess you didn't see me—ha?

HJALMAR. No, but they told me you'd come through —so I thought I'd try to catch up with you.

EKDAL. Hmm, nice of you, Hjalmar. Who were they, all those people?

HJALMAR. Oh, all kinds. Chamberlain Flor and

Chamberlain Balle, and Chamberlain Kaspersen, and Chamberlain—so-and-so— Oh, I don't know—

EKDAL (*Nodding.*) Hear that, Gina! Nothing but Chamberlains!

GINA. Yes, I guess it's pretty fancy in that house now.

HEDVIG. Did the Chamberlains sing, Papa? Or did they read something aloud?

HJALMAR. No, they just talked a lot of nonsense. And then they wanted me to recite for them; but they didn't get me to do it.

EKDAL. They didn't, huh?

GINA. You could have done that for 'em.

HJALMAR. No, you shouldn't be too eager to lick everybody's boots. (*Walks about the room.*) I'm not, anyway.

EKDAL. No, no; Hjalmar isn't such an easy mark.

HJALMAR. I don't know why I should let them impose on me to do the entertaining when I go out once in a while. Let the others make an effort. There are those fellows traipsing from one dinner to another, stuffing themselves and guzzling, day in and day out. Well, let them make themselves useful and earn their dinners.

GINA. But you didn't tell 'em that, did you?

HJALMAR (*Hums.*) Hum-hum-hum.— They heard a little bit of everything.

EKDAL. And that was to the Chamberlains themselves?

HJALMAR. Why not? (*Casually.*) And later we got into a little argument about Tokay.

EKDAL. Tokay wine, my boy? That's a fine wine.

HJALMAR (*Stopping.*) It *can* be fine. But let me tell you, not all the vintages are equally good. It all depends on how much sunshine the grapes have had.

GINA. My, you know everything. You sure do, Hjalmar.

EKDAL. And they started arguing about it?

HJALMAR. They were going to try; but then they were told it was the same with Chamberlains—that with them, too, not all of them were good. That's what they were told.

GINA. My, what you can think of to say!

EKDAL. He-hee! So that's what you dished up to them?

HJALMAR. Right in the face.

EKDAL. Hear that, Gina? He told the Chamberlains right to their faces.

GINA. Imagine that! Right to their faces!

HJALMAR. Yes, but I don't want any mention of it. You don't talk about things like that. And anyway, it was all very friendly, of course. They're a good-natured bunch; why should I hurt them—no!

EKDAL. Right in their faces—

HEDVIG (*Flatteringly.*) What fun it is to see you in tails. You look very good in it, Papa.

HJALMAR. Yes, don't you think? I can't complain about the fit. It might have been made for me—a little tight in the armpits, maybe. Give me a hand, Hedvig. (*He takes off the coat.*) I guess I'll put on my jacket. Where is it, Gina?

GINA. Here.

(*She brings the jacket and helps him.*)

HJALMAR. There! Don't forget to give the dress suit back to Molvik first thing in the morning.

GINA (*Laying the coat aside.*) I won't forget.

HJALMAR (*Stretching.*) Ah, this is more like home. A casual, loose-fitting outfit like this suits my personality much better. Don't you think so, Hedvig?

HEDVIG. Yes, Papa.

HJALMAR. When I pull my necktie out like this and let the ends flow—look—Ha?

HEDVIG. Yes, it looks good with the moustache and your long curly hair.

HJALMAR. I wouldn't really call it curly. I'd say rather wavy.

HEDVIG. Yes, because they really are the biggest curls.

HJALMAR. Wavy is better, I think.

HEDVIG (*After a short pause, tugging at his jacket.*) Papa!

HJALMAR. What is it?

HEDVIG. Oh, you know all right.

HJALMAR. No, I don't; I don't know what you're talking about.

HEDVIG (*Laughing and begging.*) Oh yes, Papa, don't tease me any more!

HJALMAR. Well then, what is it?

HEDVIG (*Shaking him.*) Ah, don't Papa! Give them to me. You know, all the good things you promised me. You know!

HJALMAR. Oh—how could I forget it?

HEDVIG. You're just joking, Papa! That isn't nice of you. Where are they?

HJALMAR. But I did forget. It's the truth. Wait a minute! I have something else for you, Hedvig.

(*Goes and looks through the pockets of the coat.*)

HEDVIG (*Jumping up and down, and clapping her hands.*) Oh, Mother, Mother!

GINA. There, you see; if you'll just have a little patience—

HJALMAR (*With a piece of paper.*) Here we are.

HEDVIG. That? That's just a piece of paper.

HJALMAR. It's the bill of fare, dear; the whole bill of fare. Here, this says "Menu"—that means bill of fare.

HEDVIG. Don't you have anything else?

HJALMAR. I forgot the other things, I tell you. But believe me, these delicacies don't amount to much. You sit down at the table now and read the list and later on, I'll tell you how they tasted. Here you are, Hedvig.

HEDVIG (*Choking down her tears.*) Thank you.

(*She sits, but doesn't read.* GINA *makes signs to her, but* HJALMAR *notices it.*)

HJALMAR (*Walking up and down.*) It's unbelievable what things the head of a family is supposed to remember. And if you forget even the least thing— right away it's sulky faces. Well, you can get used to that, too. (*Steps by the stove near his father.*) Did you take a look in there tonight, Father?

EKDAL. Well, naturally. She's in the basket.

HJALMAR. Really? She has gotten into the basket. So she's used to it.

EKDAL. I told you she would. But now, you see, there are some little things that—

HJALMAR. Some improvements, yes.

EKDAL. But they've got to be made, my boy.

HJALMAR. Yes, let's talk a bit about those improvements, Father. Come here, let's sit on the sofa.

EKDAL. All right. Hmm, I'll fill my pipe first— Looks like I'd better clean it out, too. Hmm.

(*He goes into his room.*)

GINA (*Smiling, to* HJALMAR.) He's goin' to clean his pipe!

HJALMAR. Oh well, Gina, let him—the poor, broken old man. Yes, those improvements—we'd better get them out of the way tomorrow.

GINA. I'm afraid you won't have time tomorrow, Hjalmar.

HEDVIG (*Breaking in.*) Oh yes, he will, Mother!

GINA. —Remember them prints that have to be retouched. They keep callin' for 'em.

HJALMAR. I see. It's those prints again! Don't worry; they'll be finished. Do you have any new orders?

GINA. No, I'm sorry to say. Tomorrow I don't have anything but them two portraits, you know.

HJALMAR. Is that all? Oh well, of course, if people don't make an effort—

GINA. What do you want me to do? I put all the ads in the papers we can afford.

HJALMAR. Oh, the papers, the papers. You can see how much good that does. I don't suppose there's been anybody to look at the room, either?

GINA. No, not yet.

HJALMAR. That's to be expected. When people don't go after things—you don't get anywhere unless you really try, Gina!

HEDVIG (*Coming to him.*) Do you want me to get your flute, Papa?

HJALMAR. No, I don't want it. *I* don't need any pleasures in this world. (*He wanders about.*) I'll work tomorrow; don't you worry about that. I'll work as long as my strength holds out.

GINA. But, dear! Hjalmar! That wasn't what I meant.

HEDVIG. Papa, how about a bottle of beer?

HJALMAR. No, never mind. You don't have to get anything for me—(*He stops.*) Beer? Did you say beer?

HEDVIG (*Gaily.*) Yes, Papa; nice cold beer.

HJALMAR. Well—if it means so much to you, go ahead and get me a bottle.

GINA. Yes, do; then we'll all be cosy.

(HEDVIG *runs towards the kitchen door.*)

HJALMAR (*By the stove, stops her; looks at her; takes her head in his hands, and presses her to him.*) Hedvig, Hedvig!

HEDVIG (*With tears of joy.*) Oh, you sweet, nice papa!

HJALMAR. No, don't call me that. Here I've been sitting, stuffing myself at a rich man's table—sitting there wallowing at a table groaning with—! And still I didn't even—!

GINA (*Sitting at the table.*) Hjalmar, don't, don't.

HJALMAR. Yes. But you mustn't hold it against me. You know how much I love you anyway.

HEDVIG (*Throws her arms around him.*) And we love you so much—so much, Papa.

HJALMAR. If I do seem unreasonable every once in a while, then—oh, well—remember that I'm a man who's overwhelmed by a sea of sorrows. Well! (*He *wipes his eyes.*) No beer at a moment like this. Give me my flute.

(HEDVIG *runs to the bookcase and gets the flute.*)

HJALMAR. Thank you. Like this, yes. With my flute in my hand and you two beside me—! (HEDVIG *sits at the table with* GINA. HJALMAR *walks back and forth and begins vigorously, playing a Bohemian folk dance, in a slow elegiac tempo, and with much feeling. Then he breaks off playing, holds out his left hand to* GINA *and says emotionally:*) I don't care how stifling and shabby it is here, Gina; it's still home. And I'll say this: it's good to be here.

(*He begins to play again; almost immediately there is a knock at the hall door.*)

GINA (*Rising.*) Shhhh, Hjalmar—I think there's somebody at the door.

HJALMAR (*Placing the flute on the bookcase.*) Now what?

(GINA *goes to the door.*)

GREGERS (*In the hall.*) Pardon me—

GINA (*Falling back a little.*) Oh!

GREGERS. Is this where Mr. Ekdal lives—the photographer?

HJALMAR (*Goes toward the door.*) Gregers! So you came anyway. Well, come on in, then.

GREGERS (*Coming in.*) I told you I was going to come to see you.

HJALMAR. But tonight? Did you leave the party?

GREGERS. The party—and my father's house, too. Good evening, Mrs. Ekdal. I don't know if you recognise me?

GINA. Oh yes; it isn't hard to remember young Mr. Werle.

GREGERS. No, that's right. I look like my mother; and I'm sure you remember her.

HJALMAR. Did you say you'd left home?

GREGERS. Yes, I moved to a hotel.

HJALMAR. I see. Well, now that you're here, take off your coat and have a seat.

GREGERS. Thanks.

(*He takes off his overcoat. He has changed his clothes, and is wearing a simple grey suit of a provincial cut.*)

HJALMAR. Here, on the sofa. Make yourself comfortable.

(GREGERS *sits on the sofa,* HJALMAR *in a chair by the table.*)

GREGERS (*Looking around.*) So here's where you keep yourself, Hjalmar—this is where you live.

HJALMAR. This is the studio—you can see that, I suppose—

GINA. It's bigger, so we usually stay in here.

HJALMAR. We had a better place before, but this apartment has one big advantage—it has fine front rooms with lots of light.

GINA. And we have a room on the other side of the hall that we can rent out.

GREGERS (*To* HJALMAR.) I see—you've roomers, too.

HJALMAR. No, not yet. It isn't as easy as all that; you have to be on your toes. (*To* HEDVIG.) How about that beer, Hedvig?

(HEDVIG *nods and goes out into the kitchen.*)

GREGERS. So that's your daughter?

HJALMAR. Yes, that's Hedvig.

GREGERS. And she's your only child?

HJALMAR. Yes, she's the only one. She's the greatest joy we have in the world and— (*He lowers his voice.*) She's also our deepest sorrow, Gregers.

GREGERS. What do you mean?

HJALMAR. Just what I said. There's grave danger that she'll lose her eyesight.

GREGERS. Go blind?

HJALMAR. Yes. She has only the first symptoms so far, and everything may be all right for a while yet. But the doctor has warned us. It's coming. Nothing can stop it.

GREGERS. How horrible! What does it come from?

HJALMAR (*Sighs.*) I suppose she's inherited it.

GREGERS (*Startled.*) Inherited?

GINA. Hjalmar's mother had weak eyes, too.

HJALMAR. That's what my father says; I can't remember her, of course.

GREGERS. The poor child. How does she take it?

HJALMAR. Naturally we haven't the heart to tell her. She doesn't know she's in any danger. She's as happy and carefree as a little bird—flying straight into a life of endless night. (*Overcome.*) Oh, it's such a crushing burden to me, Gregers.

(HEDVIG *brings in a tray with beer and glasses, places it on the table.*)

HJALMAR (*Strokes her hair.*) Thank you, thank you, darling.

(HEDVIG *puts her arm around his neck and whispers in his ear.*)

HJALMAR. No. We don't want any bread and butter just now. (*He looks at* GREGERS.) Perhaps Gregers would like a piece.

GREGERS (*With a gesture of refusal.*) No. No, thank you.

HJALMAR (*Still melancholy.*) Well, maybe you'd better bring in a little. If you have a crust, that's all I want. And put plenty of butter on it, will you.

(HEDVIG *nods, pleased, and goes out to the kitchen again.*)

GREGERS (*Who has followed her with his eyes.*) She looks healthy enough.

GINA. Yes, she's all right except for that, thank God.

GREGERS. She's going to look like you someday, Mrs. Ekdal. How old is she?

GINA. She'll be just fourteen soon; it's her birthday day after tomorrow.

GREGERS. In that case she's pretty big for her age.

GINA. Yes, she's really shot up this last year.

GREGERS. Watching children grow up makes you realize how old you're getting—How long have you been married now?

GINA. We've been married for—umhum—it'll soon be fifteen years.

GREGERS. Really? Has it been that long?

GINA (*With sudden attention; looks at him.*) Yes—certainly it has.

HJALMAR. Oh yes, of course. Fifteen years, short a few months. (*With a change of tone.*) They must have been long years for you, up there at the factory, Gregers.

GREGERS. They were long while I was living them. Now, afterwards, I hardly know what's happened to the time.

(OLD EKDAL *comes in from his room, without his pipe, but with his old-fashioned uniform cap on; he is a little unsteady on his feet.*)

EKDAL. All right, my boy. Now, Hjalmar, let's sit down and talk about this—hmm—what was it now?

HJALMAR (*Crossing to him.*) There's somebody here, Father—Gregers Werle. I don't know if you remember him.

EKDAL (*Looks at* GREGERS, *who has gotten up.*) Werle? The son—is that who it is? What does he want with me?

HJALMAR. Nothing; it's me he came to see.

EKDAL. Oh, well—then, there's nothing wrong?

HJALMAR. No, no, of course not.

EKDAL (*Waving his arm.*) It's not that, you see; I'm not afraid, but—

GREGERS (*Going to him.*) I just wanted to bring you greetings from your old hunting-grounds, Lt. Ekdal.

EKDAL. Hunting-grounds?

GREGERS. Yes, up at Highdale, around the factory.

EKDAL. Oh, up there. Yes, I used to know my way around up there.

GREGERS. You were quite a hunter then.

EKDAL. So I was, yes. That's true enough. You're looking at my cap. I don't ask anybody's permission to wear it in here. Just so I don't go on the street with it—

(HEDVIG *brings a plate of bread and butter; puts it on the table.*)

HJALMAR. Sit down, Father, and have a glass of beer. Here you are, Gregers.

(EKDAL *mumbles and makes his way, stiff-legged, to the sofa.* GREGERS *sits on the chair nearest him,* HJALMAR *on the other side of* GREGERS. GINA *sits at a little distance from the table, sewing.* HEDVIG *stands by her father.*)

GREGERS. Remember, Lt. Ekdal, when Hjalmar and I used to come up to visit you in the summertime, and at Christmas?

EKDAL. Did you? No, no, no; I can't remember that at all. But I sure enough was a first-class hunter. And bears, I've shot them, too. I've shot nine, no less.

GREGERS (*Looking at him sympathetically.*) And now you never go hunting any more?

EKDAL. Oh, I wouldn't say that, my boy. I go hunting every once in a while. Well, not quite that way. Because, you see—the woods—the woods, the woods—! (*He drinks.*) How are the woods up there now? Are they good?

GREGERS. Not as fine as in your day. They've been thinned out pretty badly.

EKDAL. Thinned out? (*Lowering his voice, almost frightened.*) That's a dangerous thing to do. It has consequences. The woods will be revenged.

HJALMAR (*Filling his glass.*) Here you are—have a little more, Father.

GREGERS. How can a man like you—a man who belongs in the open—live right here in the center of a stifling town, walled in like this?

EKDAL (*Laughs a little, and throws a side glance at* HJALMAR.) Oh, it isn't so bad here. Not bad at all.

GREGERS. But the things that used to be a part of you—the cool, sweeping wind, the free life in the woods and the mountain meadows, with the birds and the animals—

EKDAL (*Smiles.*) Hjalmar, shall we show him?

HJALMAR (*Quickly, a little embarrassed.*) Oh no, no, Father; not tonight.

GREGERS. What does he want to show me?

HJALMAR. Oh, it's just something—you can see it some other time.

GREGERS (*Continuing, to* OLD EKDAL.) Well, this was what I had in mind, Lt. Ekdal, that I'd like to have you come up to the factory with me. I'll probably be going back soon. It would be easy for you to get some copying to do up there, too. And you don't really have anything here to cheer you up—and give you the feeling of home.

EKDAL (*Staring at him in amazement.*) I don't have anything to—

GREGERS. Well, of course, you have Hjalmar; but after all he has his own family. And a man like you, who's always had such a passion for freedom and the wilderness—

EKDAL (*Striking the table.*) Hjalmar, now he's got to see it!

HJALMAR. But Father, do you think we'd better? It's dark and—

EKDAL. Oh, nonsense! There's plenty of moonlight. (*He stands.*) He's got to see it, I tell you. Let me get by, will you! Come on and help me, Hjalmar.

HEDVIG. Oh yes, please do, Papa!

HJALMAR (*Rising.*) Well, all right then.

GREGERS (*To* GINA.) What's this all about?

GINA. Oh, it's nothing much.

(EKDAL *and* HJALMAR *have gone to the rear wall and each slides one of the double doors open.* HEDVIG *helps the old man.* GREGERS *remains standing by the sofa.* GINA *sits undisturbed, sewing. Through the open doorway is seen a large, elongated, irregular garret with many half-hidden nooks and crannies. It is broken by a couple of chimneys. Bright moonlight shining through several skylights illuminates parts of the great room; other portions are in deep shadow.*)

EKDAL (*To* GREGERS.) Come closer, my boy, it's all right.

GREGERS (*Crossing to them.*) Well, what is it?

EKDAL. Take a look. Hmm.

HJALMAR (*A little embarrassed.*) This belongs to my father, you understand.

GREGERS (*By the door, looking into the garret.*) Why, you keep chickens, Lt. Ekdal.

EKDAL. I should think we do. They've gone to roost now. But you ought to see those chickens by daylight.

HEDVIG. And then there's—

EKDAL. Shhh—shh! Don't tell him yet.

GREGERS. And you've got pigeons, too, I see.

EKDAL. Maybe. Maybe we do at that. They have their boxes up there under the eaves because pigeons like to nest way up in the air, you know.

HJALMAR. They aren't all just ordinary pigeons.

EKDAL. Ordinary! No, I should say not! We have tumblers, and we've got a couple of pouters, too. But come here! See that hutch over there by the wall?

GREGERS. Yes, what's it for?

EKDAL. That's where we keep the rabbits at night, my boy.

GREGERS. Oh. You've got rabbits, too?

EKDAL. Why, hell yes, we've got rabbits! He asks if we've got rabbits, Hjalmar! Hmm! But now I'm going to show you the real thing! This is it! Move over, Hedvig. You stand right here—like that—and now look down there. Do you see a basket with straw in it?

GREGERS. Yes. And I can see there's a bird lying in the basket.

EKDAL. Hmm—a "bird"—

GREGERS. Isn't it a duck?

EKDAL (*Wounded.*) Well of course, it's a duck.

HJALMAR. But what kind of duck, do you think?

HEDVIG. It's not just an ordinary one—

EKDAL. Sh.

GREGERS. And it isn't a Muscovy either.

EKDAL. No, Mr.—Werle; it isn't a Muscovy duck, because it's a wild duck!

GREGERS. No! Really? A wild duck?

EKDAL. Ah-hah, that's what it is. That "bird" as you called it—that's the wild duck, that's what it is—our wild duck, my boy.

HEDVIG. Mine. Because she belongs to me.

GREGERS. And it can live up here in the attic? And grow?

EKDAL. Well, of course, she's got a trough of water to splash in, anybody would know that.

HJALMAR. Fresh water every other day.

GINA (*Turning to* HJALMAR.) Hjalmar, dear, it's gettin' cold as ice in here.

HJALMAR. Hmm, well let's close it up then. We'd better not disturb their night's rest, anyway. Give me a hand, Hedvig.

(HJALMAR *and* HEDVIG *close the doors.*)

EKDAL. Some other time you can get a good look at her. (*He sits in the easy chair by the stove.*) Oh, they're strange birds, those wild ducks, let me tell you.

GREGERS. But how did you manage to catch this one, Lt. Ekdal?

EKDAL. *I* didn't catch her. There's a certain gentleman here in town that we can thank for her.

GREGERS (*A bit startled.*) That gentleman wouldn't be my father by any chance?

EKDAL. Right you are. That's exactly who it is. Hmm.

HJALMAR. It's a funny thing you should guess that, Gregers.

GREGERS. Well you told me earlier that you owed my father so much; I put two and two together—

GINA. But it wasn't Mr. Werle himself that gave us the duck—

EKDAL. He was out in a boat, you see, and took a shot at her. But your father's eyes aren't very good. Hmm. He just crippled her.

GREGERS. I see. Just peppered a bit.

HJALMAR. Yes, she got a couple of bird-shot in her.

HEDVIG. Under her wing, so she couldn't fly.

GREGERS. I see. So I suppose she dove to the bottom?

EKDAL (*Sleepily, thickly.*) Naturally. They always do, those wild ducks. Beat it for the bottom as far down as they can get, my boy—and grab a good hold on the seaweed—and all that damned stuff that grows down there. And they don't ever come up again.

GREGERS. But, Ekdal, your wild duck did come up again.

EKDAL. He has an awful smart dog, your father has. And that dog—he dove right down after her and brought her up.

GREGERS (*Turning to* HJALMAR.) And then he gave it to you?

HJALMAR. Not right away. He took her home first. But she didn't do well there; so he told Pettersen to put an end to her—

EKDAL (*Half asleep.*) Hmm—m'yah—Pettersen— that fathead—

HJALMAR (*Lowering his voice.*) That's the way we got her, you see. My father knows Pettersen a little, and when he heard about the duck he talked him into giving her to us.

GREGERS. And it gets along very well in the attic there.

HJALMAR. Yes, you wouldn't believe it, Gregers. She's gotten fat. Well, she's been in there so long now, that she's forgotten her natural wild life; and it all depends on that.

GREGERS. I guess you're right there, Hjalmar. Just don't ever let her get a glimpse of the sky and the sea—but I guess I'd better not stay any longer; I think your father's asleep.

HJALMAR. Oh, as far as that's concerned—

GREGERS. Say, that's right—you mentioned you had a room for rent—a vacant room?

HJALMAR. Yes; why? Do you know of anybody?

GREGERS. May *I* have it?

HJALMAR. You?

GINA. But—*you*, Mr. Werle—

GREGERS. May I have it? I'll move in first thing tomorrow morning.

HJALMAR. Why yes, we'll be happy to—

GINA. But, Mr. Werle, that's no kind of a room for you.

HJALMAR. Gina! How can you say that?

GINA. Because that room ain't big enough or light enough neither, and—

GREGERS. That doesn't make any difference, Mrs. Ekdal.

HJALMAR. I think it's a pretty nice room, and the furniture isn't so bad.

GINA. But remember them two downstairs.

GREGERS. Who are they?

GINA. Oh, one of 'em's been a tootor—

HJALMAR. A Mr. Molvik—

GINA. And then a doctor, by the name of Relling.

GREGERS. Relling? I've met him. He practised for a while up at Highdale.

GINA. They're a pretty wild pair of gentlemen. Lots of times they go out on a binge, and then they don't come home till late at night, and they aren't always so—

GREGERS. It doesn't take long to get used to something like that. I hope to be like the wild duck—

GINA. Hmm, I think you ought to sleep on it first, anyway.

GREGERS. You'd much rather not have me in the house, wouldn't you, Mrs. Ekdal?

GINA. Good heavens, no. What makes you think that?

HJALMAR. This is a very strange way to act, Gina. (*To* GREGERS.) Are you thinking of staying in town for the time being?

GREGERS (*Putting on his coat.*) Yes, I think I'll stay here now.

HJALMAR. But not at home, with your father? What do you intend to do?

GREGERS. If I only knew that, Hjalmar—I'd be much better off. But when you have to carry such a cross as to be called "Gregers." "Gregers" and then "Werle" besides; have you ever heard anything so hideous?

HJALMAR. Oh, I don't think so at all.

GREGERS. Ugh! Agh! I'd like to spit on a fellow with a name like that. But when you've once been damned with the name Gregers Werle in this world, as I am—

HJALMAR (*Laughing.*) If you weren't Gregers Werle, what would you like to be?

GREGERS. If I could choose, before anything else I'd like to be a smart dog.

GINA. A dog!

HEDVIG (*Involuntarily.*) Oh, no!

GREGERS. Yes. A tremendously smart dog, the kind

that goes down after wild ducks when they dive to the bottom and grab hold of the tangled seaweed down in the mud.

HJALMAR. Hey, wait a minute now, Gregers—I don't understand a word of this.

GREGERS. No, I don't suppose it means anything anyway. Well, first thing tomorrow I'll move in. (*To* GINA.) I won't be any trouble; I'll do everything myself. (*To* HJALMAR.) We'll talk about the rest tomorrow. Good night, Mrs. Ekdal. (*Nods to* HEDVIG.) Good night.

GINA. Good night, Mr. Werle.

HEDVIG. Good night.

HJALMAR (*Has been lighting a candle.*) Wait a second; I'd better give you some light. I'm afraid it's dark on the stairs.

(GREGERS *and* HJALMAR *go out through the hall door.*)

GINA (*Looking before her, with her sewing in her lap.*) Wasn't that a funny thing to say, about wanting to be a dog?

HEDVIG. I'll tell you one thing, Mother—I think he meant something else by it.

GINA. And what might that have been?

HEDVIG. I don't know; but it was just as if he meant something else—all the time.

GINA. You think so? Well, it was strange enough.

HJALMAR (*Coming back.*) The light was still on. (*Blows out the candle and sets it down.*) Well, finally, a man can get a bite to eat. (*Begins to eat the bread and butter.*) There you see, Gina—if you're just on your toes—

GINA. What do you mean, on your toes?

HJALMAR. It was a good piece of luck anyway to rent the room finally. And in addition—to someone like Gregers—a good old friend.

GINA. Well, I don't know what to say.

HEDVIG. Oh Mother, you just wait and see; it'll be a lot of fun.

HJALMAR. What's the matter with you? Just a minute ago you were so eager to get it rented, and now you don't like it.

GINA. Hjalmar, if it had just been to somebody else. What do you think Mr. Werle is going to say?

HJALMAR. Old Werle? It's none of his damn business.

GINA. But it's clear as day something's gone wrong between them again, since the son's movin' out of the house. You know how they are with each other.

HJALMAR. Well, maybe, but—

GINA. And now Mr. Werle might think that you're behind it—

HJALMAR. Let him! All right, Mr. Werle's done a lot for me—I admit that. That's no reason why I should be dependent on him for the rest of my life.

GINA. But Hjalmar, dear, maybe your father will suffer for it. Maybe he'll lose the few cents that he gets from Graaberg.

HJALMAR. I might say: I wish he would! Don't you think it's a little humiliating for a man like me to see his old grey-haired father living like a beggar? But now I think the time is near. (*Takes another piece of bread and butter.*) If I really do have a mission in life, I'm going to carry it out.

HEDVIG. Oh yes, Papa, do!

GINA. Shhh! Don't wake him up!

HJALMAR (*More softly.*) I am going to carry it out, I tell you. The day will come when— And that's why it's good we've rented the room. It makes me more independent. The man who has a mission in life must be independent. (*By the easy chair, deeply moved.*) My poor old white-haired father!—You just put your faith in your Hjalmar. He's got broad shoulders— strong shoulders, anyway. Some fine day you're going to wake up and— (*To* GINA.) Maybe you don't be- lieve me?

GINA (*Rising.*) Of course, I do; but first let's see about gettin' him to bed.

HJALMAR. Yes, let's do that.

(*They take hold of the old man gently.*)

Act Three

THE SCENE: (HJALMAR EKDAL's *studio. It is morn-ing. Daylight pours through the great skylight. The curtains are open.*

AT RISE: HJALMAR *is sitting by the table, retouch-ing a photograph. Several other pictures are lying before him. After a moment,* GINA *comes in through the hall door. She is wearing her hat and coat. A covered basket hangs on her arm.*)

HJALMAR. Are you back already, Gina?
GINA. Oh yes, you've gotta keep goin'.

(*She sets her basket on the chair and takes her hat and coat off.*)

HJALMAR. Did you have a look at Gregers' room?
GINA. Uh-huh, I did. It looks real nice in there. The minute he got in the door, he really fixed it up.
HJALMAR. Oh?
GINA. Yes, he wanted to do it all himself, he said; so he was goin' to start the fire, too, and what does he do but close the damper so the whole room was full of smoke. Oh! There was a smell like a—
HJALMAR. Oh, no!
GINA. But here's the best part; of course he wanted to put out the fire, so he threw all his dirty water in the stove. The floor is soppin' with the worst mess.
HJALMAR. That's awful.
GINA. I got the janitor's wife to clean up after him

57

the pig! But it won't be fit to live in until this afternoon.

HJALMAR. What's he doing with himself in the
meantime?

GINA. He said he'd go out for a while.

HJALMAR. I dropped in on him for a minute, too—
after you'd gone.

GINA. So I heard. I hear you asked him to lunch.

HJALMAR. Oh, you know. Just a little bit of brunch.
After all, it's the first day. We couldn't very well get
out of it. You have something in the house, don't you?

GINA. I'll have to see what I can find.

HJALMAR. But be sure it isn't too meager, because
I guess Relling and Molvik are coming up, too. I just
happened to meet Relling on the stairs, you see; and
then, naturally, I felt I ought to—

GINA. I see. We're goin' to have them, too?

HJALMAR. Well, good heavens—a couple of people
more or less—it can't make much difference.

(OLD EKDAL *opens his door and looks in.*)

EKDAL. Say, listen, Hjalmar—(*Sees* GINA.) Oh!
Well—

GINA. Do you want something, Grandpa?

EKDAL. Oh no, never mind. Hmm!

(*He goes out again.*)

GINA (*Taking the basket.*) Be sure you keep an
eye on him. Don't let him go out.

HJALMAR. I will, I will.—Say, Gina, a little herring
salad would be awfully nice. I think Relling and
Molvik were out on a binge last night.

GINA. Just so they don't come before I'm ready—

HJALMAR. No, no, they won't; take your time.

GINA. Well, all right; and you can always do a little work in the meantime.

HJALMAR. Can't you see? I'm sitting here working! I'm working as hard as I can.

GINA. Because then that'll be out of the way, you see.

(*She goes out to the kitchen with the basket. HJALMAR sits, for a moment, dabbing at the photograph. He does it slowly and with distaste.*)

EKDAL (*Peeks in. Looks around the studio and says softly:*) Are you busy, Hjalmar?

HJALMAR. What does it look like? I'm sitting here struggling with these pictures—

EKDAL. Well, well, never mind—if you're that busy, then—Hmm!

(*He goes back to his room; the door remains open.*)

HJALMAR (*Continues for a while in silence; then he puts the brush down and goes to the open door.*) Are *you* busy, father?

EKDAL (*Grumbling, within.*) If you're busy, I'm busy, too—hmm!

HJALMAR. Oh well, all right.

(*He goes back to his work again.*)

EKDAL (*After a moment, appears in the door again.*) Hmm; look here, Hjalmar, I'm not *that* busy.

HJALMAR. I thought you were writing.

EKDAL. Well, what the hell! Can't Graaberg wait a day or two? It isn't a matter of life and death.

HJALMAR. No, and you aren't a slave either.

EKDAL. And then there's that—in there—

HJALMAR. Just what I was thinking of. You want to go in there? Shall I open the door for you?

EKDAL. It wouldn't be a bad idea.

HJALMAR (*Rising.*) Because then that would be out of the way.

EKDAL. Yes, exactly. It's got to be finished by tomorrow morning. It is tomorrow, isn't it? Hmm?

HJALMAR. Sure it's tomorrow.

(HJALMAR *and* EKDAL *each slide back one of the doors. The morning sun is shining through the skylights. Some pigeons are flying about; others are walking along the rafters, cooing. Every once in a while, the hens cackle, further back in the attic.*)

HJALMAR. All right, Father, go ahead and get started.

EKDAL (*Going in.*) Aren't you coming?

HJALMAR. Yes, you know—I think I'll— (*He sees* GINA *in the door to the kitchen.*) Who, me? No, I don't have time; I've got work to do.—Let's use our new mechanism—

(*He pulls a string, a kind of curtain slips down inside. Its lower half consists of an old piece of canvas, the upper portion is a piece of stretched fish net. Consequently, the floor of the garret can no longer be seen.*)

HJALMAR (*Going to the table.*) There! Now maybe I can sit in peace for a few minutes.

GINA. Is he goin' to mess around in there again?

HJALMAR. Would you rather he'd gone down to Mrs. Eriksen's? (*Sitting.*) Did you want anything? You said that—

GINA. I just wanted to ask you if you thought we could set the lunch table in here?

HJALMAR. Yes; I don't suppose anybody has an appointment this early.

GINA. No. I'm not expectin' anybody but the two sweethearts who're goin' to be taken together.

HJALMAR. Damn it! Why couldn't they be taken together some other day?

GINA. Don't worry, dear; I told them to come after lunch when you're takin' your nap.

HJALMAR. Oh, that's fine then. Well, all right, let's eat here.

GINA. Good; but there's no hurry about settin' the table; you can use it for a while yet.

HJALMAR. I should think you can see I'm sitting here, using it all I can!

GINA. Because then you'll be free later on, you see.

(*She goes out into the kitchen again. A short pause.*)

EKDAL (*Appearing in the attic doorway, behind the net.*) Hjalmar!

HJALMAR. Yes?

EKDAL. Afraid we're going to have to move that water trough, after all.

HJALMAR. That's what I've been saying all along.

EKDAL. Hmm—hmm—hmm.

(*He disappears again.* HJALMAR *works a while
longer; glances toward the attic and half rises.*
HEDVIG *comes in from the kitchen.*)

HJALMAR (*Sitting again quickly.*) What do you
want?

HEDVIG. I just wanted to be with you, Papa.

HJALMAR (*After a moment.*) What are you snoop-
ing around for? Are you supposed to be watching me?

HEDVIG. No, of course not.

HJALMAR. What's your mother doing out there?

HEDVIG. Mother's right in the middle of the herring
salad. (*Going to the table.*) Isn't there something I
could help you with, Papa?

HJALMAR. Oh no. I'd better do it all by myself—
as long as my strength holds out. Just don't worry,
Hedvig; as long as your father is allowed to keep his
health—

HEDVIG. Papa! You mustn't say such awful things!

(*She wanders about the room a bit; stops by the
open door, and looks into the attic.*)

HJALMAR. What's he doing, dear?

HEDVIG. I think it's supposed to be a new path up
to the water trough.

HJALMAR. He'll never be able to do that by himself!
And I'm condemned to sit here!

HEDVIG (*Going to him.*) Give *me* the brush, Papa;
I can do it.

HJALMAR. Don't be silly; you'll just ruin your eyes
with it.

HEDVIG. No, I won't. Give me the brush.

HJALMAR (*Rising.*) Well, it won't take more than a minute or two.

HEDVIG. Pooh, that won't hurt me. (*Taking the brush.*) There now! (*Sitting.*) And here's one I can copy from.

HJALMAR. But don't ruin your eyes! Do you hear me? I'm not going to be responsible. You've got to take the responsibility yourself—understand?

HEDVIG (*Retouching.*) Yes, yes, I will.

HJALMAR. You're a good girl, Hedvig. Just for a couple of minutes, you understand.

(*He slips around the edge of the curtain and into the attic.* HEDVIG *sits at her work.* HJALMAR *and* EKDAL *can be heard arguing in the attic.*)

HJALMAR (*Appears behind the net.*) Hedvig— would you please give me the pair of pliers on the shelf? And the crowbar. (*Turning back towards the attic.*) You just wait a minute and you'll see, Father. At least give me a chance to show you what I mean! (HEDVIG *has gotten the tools from the bookcase and pushes them through the net.*) That's fine, thank you. It is a good thing I got here when I did.

(*He leaves the doorway. The sound of their conversation and carpentering begins again.* HEDVIG *stands looking in at them. After a moment, there is a knock at the hall door. She does not hear it.*)

GREGERS (*Without hat and coat, comes in and stops near the door.*) Eh—

HEDVIG (*Turns and goes towards him.*) Good morning. Please, won't you come in?

GREGERS. Thank you. (*Looking towards the attic.*) It sounds like you've got workmen in the house.

HEDVIG. No, it's just Papa and Grandpa. I'll tell them you're here.

GREGERS. No, no; don't do that. I'd rather wait a while.

(*He sits on the sofa.*)

HEDVIG. It's so messy here—

(*She starts to remove the pictures.*)

GREGERS. Oh, just leave it. Are those pictures that are being touched up?

HEDVIG. Yes, a couple I was helping Papa with.

GREGERS. Please don't let me stop you.

HEDVIG. All right.

(*She moves the things closer to her, and sits down to work.* GREGERS, *meanwhile, looks at her in silence.*)

GREGERS. Did the wild duck sleep well last night?

HEDVIG. I guess she did, thank you.

GREGERS (*Turning towards the attic.*) It looks quite different by day from the way it did yesterday in the moonlight.

HEDVIG. Yes, it changes a lot. In the morning it's different from the way it is in the afternoon, and when it rains it looks different from when the weather's good.

GREGERS. Oh, you've noticed that, have you?

HEDVIG. Of course. You can't help it.

GREGERS. Do you like to stay in there with the wild duck, too?

HEDVIG. Yes, whenever I can.

GREGERS. But I don't suppose you have much free time; you're going to school, aren't you?

HEDVIG. No, not any more; Papa's afraid it will hurt my eyes.

GREGERS. Oh, then he's reading with you himself?

HEDVIG. Papa's promised to read with me, but he's never had time yet.

GREGERS. But isn't there anyone else to help you a little?

HEDVIG. Yes, there's Mr. Molvik; but he isn't always —well—sort of—

GREGERS. You mean he's drunk?

HEDVIG. I guess that's it.

GREGERS. Well, then, you have time for all sorts of things. And in there, I suppose, it's like another world —isn't it?

HEDVIG. Yes, it is—and there are a lot of interesting things, too.

GREGERS. Oh?

HEDVIG. There are big cabinets with books in them. And lots of the books have pictures.

GREGERS. Ah!

HEDVIG. And then there's an old desk with drawers and flaps, and a big clock with figures that come popping out. But the clock doesn't run any more.

GREGERS. So time is standing still in there—with the wild duck.

HEDVIG. Yes. And then there are old paint-boxes and things like that. And all the books.

GREGERS. And you read them?

HEDVIG. Oh, yes, whenever I can. Most of them are

in English, and I don't understand that. But then I can always look at the pictures.—There's a great big book called *Harrison's History of London*. I guess it's about a hundred years old; and there's an awful lot of pictures in that. In the front, there's a picture of Death with an hourglass and a young lady. I think that's awful. But then there are all the other pictures with churches and castles and streets and big ships sailing on the ocean.

see's herself

GREGERS. Where did you get all those odd things?

HEDVIG. Oh, an old sea captain lived here once. He brought them home with him. They called him "The Flying Dutchman." And that's kind of funny because he wasn't a Dutchman at all.

GREGERS. He wasn't?

HEDVIG. No. But finally one time he didn't come back; and so everything was just left here.

GREGERS. Look—when you're sitting in there looking at the pictures, don't you ever want to go out and see the real world itself?

HEDVIG. Oh, no! I'm always going to stay at home and help my father and mother.

GREGERS. Fixing up photographs?

HEDVIG. No, not just that. What I'd really like to do is learn to engrave pictures like the ones in the English books.

GREGERS. Hmm. What does your father have to say to that?

HEDVIG. I don't think he likes it much. He's very funny about those things. Can you imagine, he keeps saying that I ought to learn to weave baskets and mats! But I don't see how there can be anything in that.

GREGERS. I don't either.

HEDVIG. But Father is right when he says that if I'd learned to weave baskets, I could have made the new one for the wild duck.

GREGERS. That's right, you could. And you're the one that should have done it, too.

HEDVIG. Yes, because she's my wild duck.

GREGERS. Of course she is.

HEDVIG. Um-hum. *I* own her. But Papa and Grandpa can borrow her as often as they want to.

GREGERS. Oh? What do they do with her?

HEDVIG. Oh, they putter around with her, and build for her, and things like that.

GREGERS. I'm not surprised. I suppose the wild duck is the aristocrat of the attic.

HEDVIG. She certainly is; because she's a real wild bird. And you can't help feeling sorry for her; she doesn't have anybody to keep her company, poor thing.

GREGERS. She has no family, like the rabbits—

HEDVIG. No. And the hens, too; lots of them were little chicks together. But she's left all her family behind. And then, of course, it's very mysterious about the wild duck. Nobody knows who she is, and nobody knows where she comes from even.

GREGERS. And she's been down in the depths of the sea.

HEDVIG (*Looks quickly at him, suppresses a smile and asks:*) Why do you say "depths of the sea"?

GREGERS. What else should I say?

HEDVIG. You could have said "the sea floor" or "the bottom of the sea."

GREGERS. Can't I just as well say "the depths of the sea"?

HEDVIG. Yes, but it sounds so strange to me when someone else says "the depths of the sea."

GREGERS. Why? Tell me.

HEDVIG. No, I won't. It's so silly.

GREGERS. I'm sure it isn't. Tell me why you smiled.

HEDVIG. It's because—always—when I think of the place in there, all of a sudden, it always seems to me as if the best name of the whole room and everything is "the depths of the sea."—But that's silly.

GREGERS. No! Don't say that.

HEDVIG. Yes, because it's really just an attic.

GREGERS (*Looks fixedly at her.*) Are you so sure of that?

HEDVIG (*Surprised.*) That it's an attic?

GREGERS. Yes. Are you—sure?

(HEDVIG *is silent and stares at him open-mouthed.* GINA *comes in from the kitchen with dishes for the table.*)

GREGERS (*Rising.*) I'm afraid I'm a little early.

GINA. Oh well, you've gotta be some place; and anyway, it'll be ready soon. Clear the table, Hedvig.

(HEDVIG *removes her things from the table; she and* GINA *set it for lunch during the following.* GREGERS *sits in an easy chair and leafs through an album.*)

GREGERS. I hear you know how to retouch photographs, Mrs. Ekdal.

GINA (*With a side glance.*) Uh-huh, I do.

GREGERS. That was pretty lucky, wasn't it?

GINA. What do you mean—lucky?

GREGERS. Since Hjalmar became a photographer, I mean.

HEDVIG. Mother can take pictures, too.

GINA. Oh yes; I've had to learn, all right.

GREGERS. Is it, by any chance, you who really runs the business?

GINA. Well, when Hjalmar doesn't have time himself—

GREGERS. I suppose his old father takes up a lot of his time?

GINA. Yes, and a man like him shouldn't have to putter around here and take pictures of just anybody who happens to come along.

GREGERS. I think so, too; but since he's once chosen that road—

GINA. You don't have to be told that Hjalmar isn't just an ordinary photographer.

GREGERS. I know. But all the same—why?

(*A shot is heard from the attic.* GREGERS *leaps to his feet.*)

What was that?!

GINA. Ugh! Now they're shootin' again.

GREGERS. Do they shoot in there, too?

HEDVIG. They go hunting.

GREGERS. What!? (*At the door to the attic.*) Are you hunting, Hjalmar?

HJALMAR (*Behind the net.*) Oh, are you here? I didn't know; I was so busy— (*To* HEDVIG.) You! Why didn't you tell us?

(*He comes into the studio.*)

GREGERS. Do you go around shooting in there in the attic?

HJALMAR (*Showing him a double-barrelled pistol.*) Oh, just with this.

GINA. Yes, you and Grandpa are goin' to have an accident sometime with that pigstol.

HJALMAR (*Annoyed.*) I believe I have told you that a weapon like this is called a pistol.

GINA. I don't see how that makes it any better.

GREGERS. So you've become a hunter, too, Hjalmar?

HJALMAR. Oh, just a little rabbit-hunting every once in a while. It's mostly for my father's sake, you know.

GINA. Men sure are funny; they always have to have something to divide themselves with.

HJALMAR (*Irritated.*) That's right; we always have to have something to *divert* ourselves with.

GINA. That's just what I'm saying—

HJALMAR. Well, hmm! (*To* GREGERS.) You see we're fortunate in that the attic is so located that nobody can hear us when we shoot. (*He puts the pistol on the top shelf of the bookcase.*) Don't touch the pistol, Hedvig! One of the barrels is still loaded; don't forget that.

GREGERS (*Looking through the net.*) I see you've got a shotgun, too.

HJALMAR. That's Father's old one. It doesn't work any more; something has gone wrong with the lock. But it's a lot of fun to have around anyway. We can take it apart and clean it every once in a while. Oil it, and put it back together again.—Of course, it's mostly my father who fools around with that.

HEDVIG (*By* GREGERS.) Now you can really see the wild duck.

GREGERS. I was just looking at her. She's drooping one wing a little, I think.

HJALMAR. Well, that's not so strange; after all, she was crippled.

GREGERS. And she drags one foot a little. Or—am I wrong?

HJALMAR. A little tiny bit, maybe.

HEDVIG. That was the foot the dog caught her by.

HJALMAR. But outside of that there isn't a thing wrong with her. And that's really remarkable when you remember she had a load of shot in her body and she's been between a dog's teeth.

GREGERS (*With a glance at* HEDVIG.) And then she's been way down in the depths of the sea—for such a long time.

HEDVIG (*Smiling.*) Yes.

GINA (*Setting the table.*) Yes, that blessed wild duck! You do everythin' but pray to her.

HJALMAR. Hmm—how's the table coming?

GINA. It'll be ready in a minute. Hedvig, you come on and help me now.

(GINA *and* HEDVIG *go out into the kitchen.*)

HJALMAR (*Lowering his voice.*) I don't think you ought to stand there looking at my father; he doesn't like it. (GREGERS *leaves the door to the attic.*) And anyway, I'd better close it up before the others come. (*He claps his hands together.*) Whh—t, Whhh—t, go away! (*He raises the net and pulls the doors together.*) These gadgets are my own invention. It really is very entertaining to have such things to fool around with, and repair when they go wrong. And besides, we have to have them; because Gina'd rather not have rabbits and chickens in the studio.

GREGERS. No, of course not. And I guess it's your wife who runs things here?

HJALMAR. I generally turn the everyday business over to her; so that, in the meantime, I can retire to the living room and think about more important things.

GREGERS. Tell me, what are those things, Hjalmar?

HJALMAR. I'm surprised you haven't asked me that before. Or maybe you haven't heard about the invention?

GREGERS. The invention? No.

HJALMAR. Oh? You haven't? Oh no, of course, up there in the wilderness—

GREGERS. You mean you've invented something?

HJALMAR. Not quite—yet; but I'm working on it. Surely you can imagine that when I decided to sacrifice myself to photography, it wasn't just to sit around taking pictures of ordinary people.

GREGERS. No, of course; your wife was just saying the same thing.

HJALMAR. I swore that if I were going to consecrate my strength to this profession, I would raise it so high that it would become not only a science but an art. And that was when I decided to make this remarkable invention.

GREGERS. And what does the invention consist of? What's it supposed to do?

HJALMAR. Well, my friend, you mustn't ask me about details yet. It takes time, you see. And I don't want you to think I'm doing it out of vanity. I'm not working for myself. No, I have my mission in mind night and day.

GREGERS. What—mission—is that?

HJALMAR. Are you forgetting the old man with the silver hair?

GREGERS. Your poor father? But what do you think you can do for him?

HJALMAR. I can wake his self-respect from the dead, as I raise the name of Ekdal to honor and distinction again.

GREGERS. So that's what your mission is?

HJALMAR. Yes, I'm going to save the shipwrecked old man. Because he *was* wrecked, in the very beginning of the storm. When these horrible investigations were taking place, he was no longer himself. That pistol over there, Gregers—that we use to shoot rabbits with—has played its part in the tragedy of our house.

GREGERS. The pistol! It has?

HJALMAR. When the sentence had been passed, and they were going to put him in prison—he had the pistol in his hand—

GREGERS. You mean he was—?

HJALMAR. Yes; but he was afraid—he was a coward. He'd already become so sick at heart, so broken, even then! Can you believe it! He, a soldier; a man who had shot nine bears, and was descended from two lieutenant colonels—well, one after the other, of course. Can you understand that, Gregers?

GREGERS. Yes, I can understand it very well.

HJALMAR. I can't. And then another time the pistol played a part in the history of our family. When he had put on the grey suit and was sitting under lock and key—oh, you have no idea how terrible a time that was for me. I kept the shades down over both of my windows. When I looked out, I saw that the sun was shining as usual. I couldn't understand it. I saw people in the street laughing and talking about unimportant things. I couldn't understand it. It seemed to me as if everything in the world ought to be at a standstill—as though eclipsed.

GREGERS. That's the way I felt, too, when Mother died.

HJALMAR. And in one of those moments, Hjalmar Ekdal pointed the pistol at his own breast.

GREGERS. You, too—thought of—

HJALMAR. Yes.

GREGERS. But you didn't shoot?

HJALMAR. No. At the crucial moment, I conquered myself. I remained alive. But I want you to know one thing: it takes courage to choose life under such circumstances.

GREGERS. Well, that depends on how you look at it.

HJALMAR. There's no question about it. But it's just as well; because my invention will soon be finished now, and when that's done, Dr. Relling thinks, just as I do, that Father can get permission to wear his uniform again. I will demand that as my only reward.

GREGERS. So it's the uniform that he—?

HJALMAR. Yes, that's what he longs and yearns for, most of all. You have no idea how my heart bleeds for him. Every time we hold a little family celebration—like our wedding anniversary, or something like that—the old man comes in dressed in his lieutenant's uniform from better days. But then, if there's a knock at the hall door—he doesn't dare be seen, you know—he runs into his room again, as fast as his old legs can carry him. It's enough to tear a son's heart to pieces.

GREGERS. When do you think this invention will be finished?

HJALMAR. Good heavens, don't ask me about details like that. You're not complete master over a thing like an invention. It depends a good deal on inspiration— on sudden insight—and it's almost impossible to figure ahead of time when that's going to happen.

GREGERS. But you *are* making progress?

HJALMAR. Of course, I am. I struggle with it every day. It fills my mind completely. Every afternoon, when I've eaten, I lock myself into the living room where I can think in peace. But people mustn't rush me; it won't do any good. That's what Relling says, too.

GREGERS. And you don't think all those things in there in the attic take you away from your work and divert your attention too much?

HJALMAR. No, no, no; just the opposite. You mustn't even say such a thing. I can't always keep concentrating on the same train of thought. It's too exhausting. I have to have a hobby that passes the time while I'm waiting. The inspiration, the insight, you see— when that does come, it will come in spite of everything.

GREGERS. My dear Hjalmar, I think you have a little of the wild duck in you.

HJALMAR. Of the wild duck? What do you mean by that?

GREGERS. You have dived down and caught hold of the tangled weeds at the bottom.

HJALMAR. Are you talking about the almost fatal shot that broke my father's wing—and mine, too?

GREGERS. No, not particularly. I wouldn't say that you are crippled. But you're lost in a poisoned marsh, Hjalmar; you're shot through with an insidious disease, and you've gone down to the bottom to die in the dark.

HJALMAR. Me? Die in the dark? Now listen here, Gregers, you've got to stop talking like that.

GREGERS. Don't get excited; I'll bring you up again. You see, I've found a mission, too. I found it yesterday.

HJALMAR. Well, all right; but leave me out of it. I assure you that—except for my melancholy, of course, which is easily explained—I'm as happy as anyone could wish to be.

GREGERS. That comes from the poison, too.

HJALMAR. No, Gregers, please, don't talk about disease and poison; I'm not used to that sort of talk at all. In my house nobody ever mentions unpleasant things to me.

GREGERS. You won't have any trouble making me believe that.

HJALMAR. It isn't good for me. And there's no marsh-poison here, as you called it. The poor photographer's home may be humble, I know—and I'm hard put to make ends meet. But I'm an inventor, Gregers— and I earn a living for my family, too. That's what lifts me above my poor circumstances.—Ah, here they come with the lunch!

(GINA and HEDVIG *bring in bottles of beer, a decanter of schnapps, glasses, and silverware. At the same time,* RELLING *and* MOLVIK *come in from the hall. Neither wears a hat or coat.* MOLVIK *is dressed in black.*)

GINA (*Putting the things on the table.*) Well, you're just in time.

RELLING. Molvik thought he could smell herring salad and then there was no holding him.—Good morning, again, Hjalmar.

HJALMAR. Gregers, I want you to meet Mr. Molvik. And Doctor—oh yes, that's right; you know Relling.

GREGERS. Yes, slightly.

RELLING. Oh, it's Mr. Werle, Junior! Yes, we've "had at it a few times" up at the Highdale factory. You've just moved in?

GREGERS. Just this morning.

RELLING. Molvik and I live right below you; so you won't have to go for doctor or preacher—if you should need anybody like that.

GREGERS. Thank you, maybe I will. There were thirteen of us at the dinner table yesterday.

HJALMAR. Oh, please, let's not talk about weird things again.

RELLING. You don't have to worry, Hjalmar. Hell, there isn't a chance it will touch you.

HJALMAR. I hope not, for the sake of my family. But let's sit down now and eat and drink and be merry.

GREGERS. Shouldn't we wait for your father?

HJALMAR. No, he wants his lunch sent in to him later. Come on!

(*The men sit at the lunch table, and eat and drink. GINA and HEDVIG pass back and forth from the studio to the kitchen, serving them.*)

RELLING. Molvik really hung one on yesterday, Mrs. Ekdal.

GINA. Oh? Again?

RELLING. Didn't you hear him when I brought him home last night?

GINA. No, I didn't.

RELLING. That's good. He was an awful mess.

GINA. Is that true, Molvik?

MOLVIK. Let's cross out last night's affair. Such things have no connection with my better self.

RELLING (*To* GREGERS.) It hits him like an inspiration. And then I have to go out on a binge with him. You see, Mr. Molvik is—daemonic.

GREGERS. Daemonic?

RELLING. Molvik is daemonic, yes.

GREGERS. Hmm.

RELLING. And daemonic natures are not made to follow a straight and narrow path through this world; they've got to get off the track once in a while.—Well, I suppose you're still sticking it out up there at that hideous black factory.

GREGERS. I've stuck it out till now.

RELLING. Did you ever manage to collect that claim you were wandering around with?

GREGERS. Claim? (*Understanding.*) Oh, I see.

HJALMAR. Have you been a claim collector, Gregers?

GREGERS. Oh, it's nothing.

RELLING. Oh yes, he has! He went around to all the homesteaders and presented something he called: "the claim of the ideal."

GREGERS. I was young then.

RELLING. You're right there; you were *very* young. And that "claim of the ideal"—you never managed to get it honored as long as *I* was up there.

GREGERS. Nor later either.

RELLING. Well, I suppose you've gotten smart enough then to knock the price down a little.

GREGERS. Not when I'm face to face with a real man.

HJALMAR. I think that's very reasonable.—A little butter, Gina.

RELLING. And a piece of pork for Molvik.

MOLVIK. Agh! Not pork!

(*There is a knock at the attic door.*)

HJALMAR. Open the door, Hedvig; your grandfather wants to come out.

(HEDVIG *goes over and opens the door a little.* OLD EKDAL *comes in with a fresh rabbit skin. She closes the door behind him.*)

EKDAL. Good morning, gentlemen! Good hunting today. Shot a big one.

HJALMAR. And you went and skinned it without waiting for me!

EKDAL. Salted it, too. It's good tender meat, rabbit meat is; and sweet; tastes like sugar. Have a good lunch gentlemen!

(*Goes into his room.*)

MOLVIK (*Rising.*) Excuse me—I can't—I have to go downst—

RELLING. Drink some soda water, man!

MOLVIK (*Hurrying.*) Ugh—ugh!

(*He disappears by the hall door.*)

RELLING (*To* HJALMAR.) Let's have a toast to the
old hunter.

HJALMAR (*Clinking glasses with him.*) To the
sportsman with one foot in the grave, yes!

RELLING. Here's to his grey hairs— (*He drinks.*)
Tell me, is his hair grey or is it white?

HJALMAR. In between, I guess. For that matter,
there isn't much of any hair left on that skull of his.

RELLING. Well—you live your span of years—even
with a wig. You know, you're a happy man, Hjalmar;
you have that beautiful mission to work for—

HJALMAR. And believe me, I work, too.

RELLING. And then you've got your nice wife, pad-
ding in and out in her felt slippers, with swaying hips,
making everything warm and comfortable for you.

HJALMAR. Yes, Gina—(*Nods to her.*)—you're a
good companion on the road of life.

GINA. Don't sit there bandying me back and forth.

RELLING. And then, your Hedvig, eh, Hjalmar?

HJALMAR (*Moved.*) My child, yes! My child before
anything else! Hedvig, come here to me. (*Stroking her
hair.*) What day is it tomorrow, dear?

HEDVIG (*Shakes him.*) Oh no, don't say anything,
Papa.

HJALMAR. It's like a knife in my heart when I think
that it's going to be so poor; just a tiny little celebration in the attic—

HEDVIG. Oh, but it will be wonderful that way!

RELLING. And you just wait until that remarkable
invention is brought into the world, Hedvig!

HJALMAR. Yes, then—then you'll see! Hedvig, I've

decided to make your future secure. You'll be taken good care of as long as you live. I'm going to demand something for you—of one kind or another—that is to be the poor inventor's only reward.

HEDVIG (*Whispers, with her arm about his neck.*) Oh Papa, you're so good to me!

RELLING (*To* GREGERS.) Well, don't you enjoy sitting, for a change, at a well-filled table in a happy family circle?

HJALMAR. Yes, these hours around the table are my favorites.

GREGERS. For my part, I don't thrive on the poisoned air of a swamp.

RELLING. Swamp poison?

HJALMAR. Oh, don't start that talk again!

GINA. There certainly ain't no poison in the air here, Mr. Werle; I air the place out every day.

GREGERS (*Leaving the table.*) The stench I'm talking about you can't air out.

HJALMAR. Stench!

GINA. Have you ever heard such a thing, Hjalmar?

RELLING. I beg your pardon—it wouldn't by any chance be you who brought it with you from the pits up there?

GREGERS. It's just like you to call what I bring into the house a stench.

RELLING (*Going to him.*) Listen, Mr. Werle, Junior: I have a strong suspicion that you're still carrying the unabridged version of that "claim of the ideal," in your back pocket.

GREGERS (*Putting his hand on his breast.*) I keep it here.

RELLING. I don't give a damn where you keep it, let

me advise you not to play the claim collector here, as long as *I'm* around.

GREGERS. And what if I do it anyway?

RELLING. I'll throw you down the stairs. Now you know.

HJALMAR (*Rising.*) Now, now Relling!

GREGERS. Go ahead, throw me out—

GINA (*Coming between them.*) I'm not goin' to let you do that, Mr. Relling. But I must say, Mr. Werle, that with the mess you made out of your stove, you shouldn't come to us and talk about bad smells.

(*A knock at the hall door.*)

HEDVIG. Mother, somebody's knocking.

HJALMAR. There! Now we're going to have strangers running in and out again!

GINA. I'll go— (*She opens the door, is startled, and draws back.*) Oh—ugh!

(MR. WERLE, *wearing a fur coat takes one step into the room.*)

WERLE. I beg your pardon; I believe my son is living here.

GINA (*Catching her breath.*) Yes.

HJALMAR (*Approaching them.*) Won't you come in, Mr. Werle?

WERLE. Thank you, I only want to talk to my son.

GREGERS. Go ahead. I'm right here.

WERLE. I want to speak to you in your room.

GREGERS. In my room? All right—

(*He starts to go.*)

GINA. Good Lord, that room ain't fit to—

WERLE. Very well, out in the hall then. I want to talk to you alone.

HJALMAR. You can do that right here, Mr. Werle. Come on, Relling, let's go into the living room.

(HJALMAR *and* RELLING *go off right.* GINA *takes* HEDVIG *into the kitchen with her.*)

GREGERS (*After a short pause.*) Well, we're alone now.

WERLE. You made some remarks last night, and since you've rented a room from the Ekdals now, I'm forced to conclude that you're thinking of making some move against me.

GREGERS. I intend to open Hjalmar Ekdal's eyes. He's going to see his position as it is—that's all.

WERLE. Is that the mission you talked about yesterday?

GREGERS. Yes. You've left me no choice.

WERLE. Am I the one, then, who has twisted your mind, Gregers?

GREGERS. You've twisted my whole life. I'm not thinking of all that business with Mother—. But I have you to thank for the fact that I'm haunted and tortured by a guilty conscience.

WERLE. Aha! It's your conscience that's bothering you, is it?

GREGERS. I should have stood up against you when you were laying the trap for Lt. Ekdal. I should have warned him; I had a pretty good idea what was up.

WERLE. Yes, that's certainly when you should have talked.

GREGERS. I didn't dare. That's how weak and cowardly I was. I was so afraid of you—not only then, but for a long time afterwards.

WERLE. I gather you've gotten over your fear.

GREGERS. Fortunately. What's been done to Old Ekdal, by me and by—others, can never be made up; but I can set Hjalmar free from the lies and silences that are about to destroy him.

WERLE. Do you think that'll be doing him a favor?

GREGERS. I'm sure of it.

WERLE. You really think Ekdal, the photographer, is man enough to thank you for a favor like that?

GREGERS. Yes! He is.

WERLE. Hmm—we'll see.

GREGERS. And besides, if I'm to go on living, I've got to find some cure for my sick conscience.

WERLE. It will never get well. Your conscience has been sick since childhood. It's an inheritance from your mother, Gregers—the only thing she left you.

GREGERS (*With a contemptuous little smile.*) Haven't you choked down your disappointment yet that she didn't bring you any money when you married her? You thought she would, didn't you?

WERLE. Let's not get off the track.—Do I understand that you're going to stick to your purpose? That you're going to put young Ekdal on what you think is the right road?

GREGERS. Yes, I am.

WERLE. Well, in that case, I could have saved myself coming up here, I don't suppose it's any use to ask you to come home again?

GREGERS. No.

WERLE. And I don't suppose you'll go into the firm either?

GREGERS. No.

WERLE. All right. Since I intend to marry again, you'll get your share of my property now.

GREGERS (*Quickly.*) I don't want it.

WERLE. You don't want it?

GREGERS. My conscience wouldn't give me a minute's peace.

WERLE (*After a short pause.*) You going back to the factory again?

GREGERS. No; I'm not working for you any more.

WERLE. But then, what are you going to do?

GREGERS. Take care of my mission, that's all.

WERLE. But what about later? How are you going to live?

GREGERS. I've saved a little out of my salary.

WERLE. And just how long is that going to last?

GREGERS. I guess it will last as long as I do.

WERLE. What's that supposed to mean?

GREGERS. I'm not going to answer any more questions.

WERLE. Then, good-bye, Gregers.

GREGERS. Good-bye.

(WERLE *goes out.*)

HJALMAR (*Looking in.*) Has he left?

GREGERS. Yes.

(HJALMAR *and* RELLING *come in;* GINA *and* HEDVIG *come in from the kitchen, too.*)

RELLING. That lunch certainly went down the drain.

GREGERS. Put on your coat, Hjalmar; I want you to take a long walk with me.

HJALMAR. I'll be glad to. What did your father want? Was it something about me?

GREGERS. Just come along. We've got to have a talk. I'll go get my coat.

(*He goes out by the hall door.*)

GINA. You shouldn't go out with him, Hjalmar.

RELLING. No, don't. Stay where you are.

HJALMAR (*Getting his hat and coat.*) What are you talking about? When a childhood friend feels the need of opening his heart to me in private—

RELLING. Oh, for God's sake—don't you understand that fellow is out of his mind, crazy, insane!

GINA. There you are! His mother used to have those nervy fits, too.

HJALMAR. The more need then, for the watchful eye of a friend. (*To* GINA.) Be sure dinner is ready in plenty of time. I'll see you later.

(*He goes out by the hall door.*)

RELLING. It's too damned bad that fellow didn't fall clear down to hell in one of those Highdale pits.

GINA. Good gracious! Why do you say that?

RELLING (*Muttering.*) Oh, I have my reasons.

GINA. Do you think young Werle is really crazy?

RELLING. No, I'm sorry to say; no crazier than most people. But he's got a disease all right.

GINA. What's wrong with him then?

RELLING. I'll tell you, Mrs. Ekdal. He suffers from an acute attack of righteousness.

GINA. Righteousness?

HEDVIG. Is that a kind of sickness?

RELLING. Uh-huh, it's our national disease; but it only appears sporadically. (*Nods to* GINA.) Thanks for the lunch.

(*He goes out by the hall door.*)

GINA (*Pacing restlessly.*) Ugh! Gregers Werle— he's always been a cold—nasty—fish.

HEDVIG (*Standing by the table and looking searchingly at her.*) Everything seems so strange all of a sudden.

Act Four

THE SCENE: (HJALMAR EKDAL'*s studio. Some pic-tures have just been taken. In the middle of the room is a camera, with a black cloth over it, on a tripod. Two chairs, a console table, and other properties are also out in the middle of the room. It is afternoon. The sun is setting. Darkness falls during the act.*

AT RISE: GINA *stands in the open hall doorway; she is holding a little box and a wet glass plate in her hands, and is speaking to someone outside.*)

GINA. Yes, yes, absolutely. When I make a promise I keep it. The first dozen will be ready on Monday. Good-bye, good-bye.

(*Someone is heard going down the stairs.* GINA *closes the door, puts the plate into the box, and slides it under the cloth into the camera.*)

HEDVIG (*Coming in from the kitchen.*) Have they left?

GINA (*Beginning to straighten up the room.*) Yes, thank God. I finally got rid of them.

HEDVIG. Why hasn't Papa come home yet?

GINA. Are you sure he ain't down at Relling's?

HEDVIG. No, he isn't there. I just ran down the kitchen stairs and asked.

GINA. And I suppose his dinner's gettin' cold, too?

HEDVIG. Yes, I can't understand it. Papa's always so careful to be home for dinner.

GINA. Oh, you'll see. He'll be home soon.

HEDVIG. I just wish he'd come, because everything's so strange all of a sudden.

GINA (*Cries out.*) Here he is!

(HJALMAR EKDAL *comes in from the hall.*)

HEDVIG (*Running to him.*) Papa! We thought you'd never get here!

GINA (*With a sidelong glance at him.*) You've been gone a long time, Hjalmar.

HJALMAR (*Without looking at her.*) Yes. Yes, it took a while.

(*He takes his overcoat off.* GINA *and* HEDVIG *want to help him; he won't allow them to.*)

GINA. Did you have somethin' to eat with Mr. Werle?

HJALMAR (*Hanging up his coat.*) No.

GINA (*Going towards the kitchen.*) I'll bring you some dinner in here then.

HJALMAR. No, never mind. I don't want to eat now.

HEDVIG (*Coming closer.*) Don't you feel well, Papa?

HJALMAR. Well? Oh yes, all right, I guess. Gregers and I took a pretty strenuous walk.

GINA. You shouldn't do that, Hjalmar. You ain't used to it.

HJALMAR. Hmm, there're a lot of things a man has to get used to in this world. (*He wanders aimlessly about.*) Has anybody been here while I was gone?

GINA. Nobody but them two sweethearts.

HJALMAR. No new orders?

GINA. No, not today.

HEDVIG. You wait and see, Papa, we'll get some tomorrow.

HJALMAR. I hope so; because tomorrow I'm really going to get down to work.

HEDVIG. Tomorrow! Don't you remember what day it is tomorrow?

HJALMAR. Oh, that's right. Well, day after tomorrow, then. From now on, I'm going to do everything myself; I'm going to be the only one working around here.

GINA. What's the good of that, Hjalmar? It'll just make you miserable. I'll take care of the photography; and you just keep working at your invention.

HEDVIG. And with the wild duck, Papa—with all the chickens, and rabbits, and—

HJALMAR. Don't talk to me about that nonsense! Beginning tomorrow I'll never set foot in the attic again.

HEDVIG. But Papa, you promised me we'd have a little party in there—

HJALMAR. Hmm, that's true. Well, all right, day after tomorrow then. That damned wild duck, I'd like to wring her neck!

HEDVIG (Cries out.) The wild duck!

GINA. I never heard of such a thing!

HEDVIG (Shaking him.) But Papa, it's my wild duck, remember?

HJALMAR. That's why I won't do it. I haven't got the heart—for your sake, Hedvig. But I feel so deeply that I ought to. I shouldn't allow anything under my roof that's been in those hands.

GINA. Well, for goodness' sake, what if Grandpa did get it from that no-good Pettersen—that's no—

HJALMAR (Wandering about.) There are certain

demands— What can I call them?—Let's say—ideal demands—certain claims, that a man can't put aside without hurting his soul.

HEDVIG (*Following him.*) But Papa, the wild duck —the poor wild duck!

HJALMAR (*Stopping.*) I told you, I won't hurt it— for your sake. Not a hair of its head will be—well, anyway, I won't hurt it. After all, there are bigger problems than that to deal with. But you ought to take your walk now, Hedvig, as usual. The twilight is just right for you.

HEDVIG. No, I don't want to go out now.

HJALMAR. Yes, do; you seem to be blinking so much; all these vapours in here aren't good for you. The air in this house is bad.

HEDVIG. All right, then, I'll run down the kitchen stairs and take a little walk. Where's my coat and hat? Oh, that's right, they're in my own room. Papa— please don't do anything to the wild duck while I'm out.

HJALMAR. I won't touch a feather on its head. (*Hugs her to him.*) You and I, Hedvig—you and I! Well, run along.

(HEDVIG *nods to her parents and goes out through the kitchen.*)

HJALMAR (*Wanders around the room, without looking up.*) Gina.

GINA. Yes?

HJALMAR. Beginning tomorrow—or, let's say, day after tomorrow—I'd like to keep the household accounts myself.

GINA. Are you goin' to do that, too?

HJALMAR. Yes, or at any rate, keep track of our income.

GINA. God help us, that won't take long.

HJALMAR. You wouldn't think so; it seems to me you make the money go an unbelievably long way. (*He stops and looks at her.*) How do you do it?

GINA. Hedvig and I don't need much.

HJALMAR. Is it true that Father gets a lot of money for the copying he does for Mr. Werle?

GINA. I don't know if it's such a lot; I don't know the price of things like that.

HJALMAR. Well, how much does he get, about? Tell me!

GINA. It's so different; I suppose it's about what he costs us, and then a little pocket money on top of that.

HJALMAR. What he costs us! And you haven't told me this before!

GINA. I couldn't do that. You were so happy thinkin' he got everything from you.

HJALMAR. And he's getting it from Mr. Werle.

GINA. Oh, well, there's plenty more where that comes from.

HJALMAR. Light the lamp, will you?

GINA (*Lighting the lamp.*) And anyway we can't tell that it's Mr. Werle himself; it might be Graaberg—

HJALMAR. Don't try to get around it with Graaberg.

GINA. Well, I don't know. I just thought—

HJALMAR. Hmm!

GINA. It wasn't me got Grandpa that copyin' job to do. You know very well it was Bertha, when she came into his house.

HJALMAR. It seems to me your voice is trembling.

GINA (*Putting the shade on the lamp.*) Is it?

HJALMAR. And your hands are shaking—or am I wrong?

GINA (*Firmly.*) Come out with it, Hjalmar. What is it he's been sayin' about me?

HJALMAR. Is it true—can it really be true that—that there was a sort of relationship between you and Mr. Werle when you were working in his house?

GINA. That isn't true. Not then, anyway. Mr. Werle was after me, that's true. And Mrs. Werle thought there was somethin' to it, and she raised an awful rumpus and hocus-pocus, and she hit me and drove me—that's just what she did, so I quit.

HJALMAR. But afterwards, then?

GINA. Well, I went home. And Mother—she wasn't as nice as you thought, Hjalmar; and she kept talking at me all the time—you know, Mr. Werle was a widower by then.

HJALMAR. Well, what then?

GINA. I guess it's better for you to know it. He didn't give me up until he'd had what he wanted.

HJALMAR (*Striking his hands together.*) And this is the mother of my child! How could you keep such a thing from me?

GINA. It was wrong of me, all right. I guess I should have told you a long time ago.

HJALMAR. Right at the start! You should have told me right at the start! Then I would have known what you were.

GINA. But would you have married me, anyway?

HJALMAR. How can you even think that?

GINA. That's just why I didn't dare tell you anything about it then. Because I was in love with you, you know; and I couldn't make myself miserable—you can understand that.

HJALMAR (*Pacing the floor.*) And this is my Hedvig's mother. And I have to know that everything I see here— (*He kicks a chair.*) my whole home—I owe to someone who enjoyed your favors first! Oh, that damned Werle!

GINA. Are you sorry about fourteen—fifteen years we've lived together?

HJALMAR (*Facing her squarely.*) Tell me, haven't you, every day, every hour, been sorry for that web of silence that you've spun around me like a spider? Answer me! Haven't you been tortured by conscience and regret?

GINA. Oh, Hjalmar dear, I've had plenty to do, thinkin' about the house, and gettin' through the day's work.

HJALMAR. You never look back at your past and question it?

GINA. No, so help me, I'd almost forgotten that old business.

HJALMAR. Oh, damn this dull, callous calm! There's something revolting about it! Can you imagine—she isn't even sorry!

GINA. Well no, tell me, Hjalmar—what would have become of you if you hadn't gotten a wife like me?

HJALMAR. Like you!

GINA. Yes; you know I've always been a little steadier and more practical than you. After all, I'm a couple of years older.

HJALMAR. What would have become of me!

GINA. Because you certainly had gotten into a lot of bad habits when you first met me; you can't deny that.

HJALMAR. So you call them "bad habits"? Oh, you don't understand how it is with a man when he's wild with sorrow and despair—especially a man with my fiery temperament.

GINA. No, maybe I don't. And I don't count that anyway. Because you did become a real good man, the minute you got a home.—And now we'd just gotten ourselves all cosy; and Hedvig and I, we were planning real soon to spend a little on ourselves, for food and clothes and things like that.

HJALMAR. Sure, in the swamp of silence.

GINA. Ugh, that rotten fellow, talkin' his way into our house!

HJALMAR. I thought we had a nice home, too. I was wrong. Now where am I going to get the strength I need to bring my invention into the world of reality? Perhaps it will die with me; and then it will be your sins, Gina, that killed it.

GINA (*Close to tears.*) Please don't say that, Hjalmar. I've never wanted to do anything but what was best for you.

HJALMAR. I ask you. Now what's going to happen to the breadwinner's dream? When I lay on the sofa in there, thinking and thinking about the invention, I had a suspicion all right that it was going to eat up my last strength. I felt it. That the day I held the patent in my hand—that day—it would be good-bye. And then I dreamt that you would be left behind, the dead inventor's rich widow.

GINA (*Wiping away her tears.*) You mustn't talk like this, Hjalmar. Dear God, don't let me live to see the day I'll be a widow!

HJALMAR. What's the difference? Everything's finished now, anyway. Everything!

(GREGERS WERLE *opens the hall door cautiously and looks in.*)

GREGERS. May I come in?

HJALMAR. Yes, come ahead.

GREGERS (*Comes in, his face beaming with happiness, and starts to hold out his hands to them.*) Well, you dear people—! (*He looks from one to the other, and whispers to* HJALMAR:) You haven't done it yet?

HJALMAR (*Aloud.*) It's done.

GREGERS. It is?

HJALMAR. I've just had the bitterest experience of my life.

GREGERS. But the most exalting too, I imagine.

HJALMAR. Well, it's over with for the time being, anyway.

GINA. God forgive you, Mr. Werle.

GREGERS (*With amazement.*) I don't understand.

HJALMAR. What don't you understand?

GREGERS. After this tremendous decision—a decision on which a whole new life is to be founded—a new way of life, a life together, in truth and with nothing held back—

HJALMAR. Yes, I know. I know all about it.

GREGERS. I was so sure, that when I came in that door, I'd be struck by the warm glow of a transfigured man and wife. And instead I see nothing but this dark, sad, unhappy—

GINA. All right!

(*Takes the shade off the lamp.*)

GREGERS. You don't want to understand me, Mrs. Ekdal. Well, no, I suppose it will take time for you.

But you, Hjalmar? Surely, you must have found a higher dedication in this great moment of reckoning.

HJALMAR. Yes, of course I have. That is, in a way—

GREGERS. Because I don't think there's anything in the world that can be compared with the joy of forgiving someone who has fallen, and lifting her up to yourself in love.

HJALMAR. Do you think it's so easy for a man to get over the bitter cup I've just drained?

GREGERS. No, for an ordinary man, maybe not. But a man like you—!

HJALMAR. Yes, yes, yes, I know. But you mustn't drive me, Gregers. It takes time, you know.

GREGERS. There's a *lot* of the wild duck in you, Hjalmar.

(RELLING *has come in from the hall.*)

RELLING. Aha! Has the wild duck come up again?

HJALMAR. The crippled victim of Mr. Werle's hunt —yes.

RELLING. Mr. Werle—? Is that who you're talking about?

HJALMAR. About him—and—ourselves.

RELLING (*In an undertone to* GREGERS.) God damn you!

HJALMAR. What did you say?

RELLING. I am giving vent to a heartfelt wish that this quack would take himself home. If he stays here, he's just the man to get both of you in a mess.

GREGERS. They won't get in a mess, Mr. Relling. I won't talk about Hjalmar—we know him. But surely she has something deep inside her, too, something true, something you can rely on—

GINA (*On the verge of tears.*) Why didn't you leave me alone, then?

RELLING (*to* GREGERS.) Would I be sticking my nose into your business if I asked what you *want* in this house?

GREGERS. I want to lay the foundation for a real marriage.

RELLING. Then you don't think Hjalmar's marriage is good enough as it is?

GREGERS. I guess it's just as good a marriage as a lot of others, unfortunately. But a *real* marriage—it hasn't become that yet.

HJALMAR. You've never been able to see the claim of the ideal, Relling.

RELLING. Baloney, my boy!—If you don't mind, Mr. Werle: How many—just make a rough estimate—how many *real* marriages have you seen in your life?

GREGERS. I'm afraid I haven't seen even one.

RELLING. Neither have I.

GREGERS. But I've seen any number of marriages of the other kind. And I've had occasion to see close at hand how much a marriage like that can destroy in two people.

HJALMAR. The whole moral foundation can slip out from under a man's feet. That's the terrible thing.

RELLING. Well, of course, I haven't ever been what you call married, so I don't dare judge those things. But this I do know, that the child is a part of the marriage, too. And you've got to leave that child alone.

HJALMAR. Ah, Hedvig!—my poor Hedvig!

RELLING. Yes, please keep Hedvig out of it. You're both grown people. In God's name, mess around with your own relationship as much as you want to. But

I'm telling you, go easy on Hedvig; otherwise you might do her terrible harm.

HJALMAR. Harm?

RELLING. Yes, or she may do herself harm—and maybe others, too.

GINA. How do you know that, Mr. Relling?

HJALMAR. Surely there's no immediate danger for her eyes is there?

RELLING. This hasn't got anything to do with her eyes. Hedvig is at a difficult age. She can take it into her head to get into all kinds of trouble.

GINA. That's right—she does, too! Lately, she's been foolin' around with the fire out in the kitchen. She says she's playin' that the house is burnin'. Lots of times I'm afraid it's really goin' to happen.

RELLING. There you are; I knew it.

GREGERS (*To* RELLING.) But how do you explain that?

RELLING (*With asperity.*) It's adolescence, man.

HJALMAR. As long as the child has me—! As long as *my* head is above earth—!

(*A knock at the door.*)

GINA. Shhh, Hjalmar; there's somebody at the door. (*She calls.*) Come in!

(MRS. SÖRBY, *wearing coat and hat, comes in.*)

MRS. SÖRBY. Good evening.

GINA (*Goes towards her.*) Why, it's you, Bertha.

MRS. SÖRBY. It certainly is. Am I interrupting anything?

HJALMAR. No, not at all. A messenger from *that* house—

MRS. SÖRBY (*To* GINA.) To be perfectly honest with you, I was hoping that I wouldn't find any of your men at home at this time. So, I just ran up for a little chat and to tell you good-bye.

GINA. Oh? Are you leaving?

MRS. SÖRBY. Yes. Early tomorrow morning—for Highdale. Mr. Werle left this afternoon. (*Casually, to* GREGERS.) He sent you his regards.

GINA. Has he really—!

HJALMAR. So Mr. Werle is gone? And you're going after him now?

MRS. SÖRBY. Yes, what do you say to that, Mr. Ekdal?

HJALMAR. Watch out—that's what I say!

GREGERS. Let me explain. My father's going to marry Mrs. Sörby.

HJALMAR. Marry her!

GINA. Oh, Bertha! At last!

RELLING (*His voice trembling a little.*) Surely this isn't true?

MRS. SÖRBY. Yes, my dear Martin, it certainly is true.

RELLING. You're going to get married again?

MRS. SÖRBY. That's the way it looks. Mr. Werle has gotten a license, and we're going to celebrate the wedding quietly up at the factory.

GREGERS. I suppose like a good stepson I'll have to wish you happiness.

MRS. SÖRBY. Thank you—if you mean it. And I hope myself that it will bring happiness to Mr. Werle and to me.

RELLING. Don't worry about that. Mr. Werle never

gets drunk, as far as I know, anyway. And I don't think he usually beats his wives, either, like the late lamented horse doctor.

MRS. SÖRBY. Oh, let Mr. Sörby rest in peace. He had his good points, too.

RELLING. I expect Mr. Werle has points that are even better.

MRS. SÖRBY. Anyway he hasn't wasted the best that's in him. The man who does that has to pay for it.

RELLING. Tonight I'm going out with Molvik.

MRS. SÖRBY. You shouldn't do that, Martin. Don't— for my sake.

RELLING. I haven't got any choice. (*To* HJALMAR.) If you want to go, come on.

GINA. No, sir. Hjalmar don't go in for that sort of dispensations.

HJALMAR (*Irritated; in an undertone.*) Oh, shut up!

RELLING. Good-bye, Mrs.—Werle.

(*He goes out into the hall.*)

GREGERS (*To* MRS. SÖRBY.) It looks as if you and Dr. Relling are pretty well acquainted.

MRS. SÖRBY. Yes, we've known each other for many years. Once we might even have made something of it.

GREGERS. It was probably a good thing for you you didn't.

MRS. SÖRBY. That's the truth. I've always been careful about acting on impulse. After all, a woman can't just throw herself away.

GREGERS. Aren't you the least bit afraid that I'm going to drop a hint to my father about this old friendship?

Mrs. Sörby. Don't you suppose I've told him myself?

Gregers. Oh?

Mrs. Sörby. Your father knows every single thing that people can say with any truth about me. I've told him everything like that. That was the first thing I did when he indicated his intentions.

Gregers. Then you're more honest than most people.

Mrs. Sörby. I've always been honest. We women get farthest with that.

Hjalmar. What do you say to that, Gina?

Gina. Oh, we women are all so different. Some are one way, and some another.

Mrs. Sörby. Well, Gina, I think it's smartest to arrange things the way I have. And Mr. Werle hasn't hidden anything either. That is the biggest bond between us. Now he can sit there and talk to me just as openly as a child. He's never had a chance to do that before. A strong, healthy man like him, all during his youth and his best years he never heard anything but moral lectures. And lots of times these lectures were about completely imaginary offences—according to what I've been told.

Gina. That's true, all right.

Gregers. If the ladies are going to get on that subject, I'd better go.

Mrs. Sörby. You might as well stay. I won't say another word. But I wanted it to be absolutely clear to you that I haven't hidden anything or done anything underhanded. Maybe it looks as if I've been very lucky; and so I have, in a way. But I still think that I'm not taking any more than I'm giving. I don't think I'll ever fail him, and I know that I can take care of him like no one else, now that he'll soon be helpless.

HJALMAR. Helpless?

GREGERS (To MRS. SÖRBY.) Never mind. Don't talk about that here.

MRS. SÖRBY. There's no use trying to hide it any longer, no matter how much he wants to. He's going blind.

HJALMAR (Startled.) Going blind? That's very strange. Is he going blind, too?

GINA. Lots of people do.

MRS. SÖRBY. And it isn't hard to imagine what that means to a business man. Well, I'll try to use my eyes for him as best I can. But I don't dare stay any longer now; I've got so many things to do.—Oh, yes, that's right, I was to tell you something, Mr. Ekdal. In case there's anything Mr. Werle can do for you, you're just to let Graaberg know.

GREGERS. I'm sure Hjalmar Ekdal can get along without that.

MRS. SÖRBY. I see. Though it doesn't seem to me that at other times he—

GINA. No, Bertha, Hjalmar doesn't need to take anything from Mr. Werle now.

HJALMAR (Slowly and emphatically.) Please give my regards to your future husband, and tell him that I intend, in the near future, to go to Mr. Graaberg—

GREGERS. What! Do you mean that?

HJALMAR. —To go to Mr. Graaberg, I say, and ask for an accounting of the sum I owe his employer. I will pay this debt of honor— (He laughs.) That's what's called "a debt of honor." But enough of that, I'm going to pay it all with five percent interest.

GINA. My God, Hjalmar dear, we haven't got the money for that.

HJALMAR. Will you tell your future husband that I'm working tirelessly at my invention? Will you tell him that the one thing that keeps me going at this exhausting labor is the wish to be rid of an embarrassing burden of debt? That's why I'm creating this invention. The entire proceeds are to be used to free me from my pecuniary obligations to your future husband.

MRS. SÖRBY. It looks as if *something* has happened in this house.

HJALMAR. Something certainly has!

MRS. SÖRBY. Well, good-bye then. I still had a few things to talk to you about, Gina, but they'll have to wait until another time. Good-bye.

(HJALMAR *and* GREGERS *bow in silence.* GINA *goes to the door with* MRS. SÖRBY.)

HJALMAR. Not beyond the door, Gina! (MRS. SÖRBY *goes;* GINA *closes the door after her.*) That's that, Gregers; now I've gotten rid of that miserable debt.

GREGERS. Soon, anyway.

HJALMAR. I believe you can call my stand correct.

GREGERS. You're the man I've always thought you were.

HJALMAR. Under certain circumstances it's impossible to deny the claim of the ideal. As the head of a family, however, I find myself writhing and groaning under it. You understand it's no joke for a poor man to be forced to clear up a debt of long standing. A debt that, as you might say, has been covered with the dust of years. But never mind: the Man in me demands his rights, too.

GREGERS (*Putting a hand on* HJALMAR'S *shoulder.*) My dear Hjalmar—now, wasn't it good I came?

HJALMAR. Yes.

GREGERS. Isn't it fine to have everything brought into the open?

HJALMAR (*A little impatiently.*) Yes, yes, of course. But there is one thing that shocks my sense of justice.

GREGERS. What's that?

HJALMAR. It's that—well, I don't know if I dare express myself so frankly about your father.

GREGERS. Don't worry about me in the least.

HJALMAR. Well, all right. You see, the way I feel is this: there's something revolting about the thought that now it won't be I, but he, who will experience the real marriage.

GREGERS. How can you say such a thing?

HJALMAR. Oh yes, it will. Your father and Mrs. Sörby are about to enter into a marriage built on absolute trust. Built on a complete and unreserved frankness on both sides. They're not hiding anything from each other, they have no secrets; they have given each other, if I may express myself so, mutual absolution.

GREGERS. Well, so what?

HJALMAR. Well, the whole thing is right there. It is just that sort of thing that has to be overcome in order to found a real marriage. You said so yourself.

GREGERS. But it's in an entirely different way, don't you see, Hjalmar? Surely you're not going to compare either yourself or her with those two—? Oh, you know what I mean.

HjALMAR. But I can't get away from the fact that there's something shocking in all this. It looks exactly as if there isn't any justice in the world at all.

GINA. Oh, no, Hjalmar; good Lord, you mustn't say such a thing!

GREGERS. Hmm; let's not get on questions like that.

HjALMAR. But on the other hand, it almost seems as if I can make out the guiding finger of fate after all. He is going blind.

GINA. Oh, maybe that isn't so sure.

HjALMAR. There's no doubt about it. *We* oughtn't to doubt it at any rate. Because just retribution lies in that very fact. In his time he has blinded an innocent fellow being—

GREGERS. I'm sorry to say he has blinded many.

HjALMAR. And now the One without mercy, the mysterious One, comes and demands Mr. Werle's own eyes.

GINA. Oh no! Aren't you afraid to say such an ugly thing! You scare me!

HjALMAR. It's good for you to go into the night side of life, once in a while.

(HEDVIG *comes in from the hall, happy and breathless. She is wearing hat and coat.*)

GINA. Are you back already?

HEDVIG. Yes, I didn't want to walk any more. And it was a good thing; because I met somebody at the front door.

HjALMAR. I suppose it was that Mrs. Sörby.

HEDVIG. Yes.

HjALMAR (*Pacing up and down.*) I hope it's the last time you've seen her.

(*There is a silence.* HEDVIG *looks unhappily from one to the other as if trying to sense their mood.*)

HEDVIG (*Coming closer to* HJALMAR; *ingratiatingly.*) Papa?

HJALMAR. Yes—what is on your mind, Hedvig?

HEDVIG. Mrs. Sörby brought me something.

HJALMAR (*Stops.*) Something for *you?*

HEDVIG. Yes, I'm not supposed to open it till tomorrow.

GINA. Bertha has always had a little something for you on your birthday--

HJALMAR. What is it?

HEDVIG. I can't tell you now. Mother is supposed to give it to me in bed tomorrow morning.

HJALMAR. I'm always left out of your little secrets!

HEDVIG (*Quickly.*) You can see it. It's a big letter.

(*Takes the letter out of her coat pocket.*)

HJALMAR. A letter, too?

HEDVIG. Yes, that's all there is now. I guess I'll get the rest later. But just think—a letter! I've never gotten a letter before. And it says "Miss" on the outside. (*She reads.*) "Miss Hedvig Ekdal." That's me!

HJALMAR. Let me see it.

HEDVIG (*Gives it to him.*) There it is.

HJALMAR. That's Mr. Werle's handwriting.

GINA. Are you sure of that, Hjalmar?

HJALMAR. Look for yourself.

GINA. How would I know?

HJALMAR. Hedvig—may I open the letter—and read it?

HEDVIG. Yes, of course, if you want to.

GINA. No, not tonight, Hjalmar. That's supposed to be for tomorrow.

HEDVIG (*Softly.*) Oh, can't you let him read it? I'm sure it's something good, and then he'll be happy, and then everything will be all right again.

HJALMAR. I may open it then?

HEDVIG. Yes, please do, Papa. It'll be fun to find out what's in it.

HJALMAR. Very well. (*He opens the letter, takes a paper out, reads it through, and seems to be bewildered.*) What's this—?

GINA. Well, what's it say?

HEDVIG. Yes, Papa,—tell us!

HJALMAR. Be quiet. (*He reads it through once more; he has grown pale, but speaks calmly.*) It's a deed of gift, Hedvig.

HEDVIG. Is it? What am I getting?

HJALMAR. Read for yourself.

(HEDVIG *goes to the lamp and reads for a while.*)

HJALMAR (*In a low voice, clenching his hands.*) The eyes! The eyes—and now this letter!

HEDVIG (*Stops reading.*) Well, it seems to me it's Grandpa who's going to get it.

HJALMAR (*Taking the letter from her.*) You, Gina —do you understand this?

GINA. You know I don't know anything. What is it?

HJALMAR. Mr. Werle writes to Hedvig that her old grandfather doesn't need to bother about the copying any more, but that from now on he can draw a hundred a month from the office—

GREGERS. Aha!

HEDVIG. A *hundred*, Mother! I read it.

GINA. That'll be fine for Grandpa.

HJALMAR. —A hundred as long as he needs it— that means of course, until he dies.

GINA. Well, that takes care of him, poor old fellow.

HJALMAR. But then comes the real thing. I guess you didn't read that, Hedvig. Afterwards that gift is transferred to you.

HEDVIG. To me? All of it?

HJALMAR. You're assured of the same amount for the rest of *your* life. You do hear that, Gina?

GINA. Yes, yes, I hear it.

HEDVIG. Oh my—all that money for me! (*Shakes* HJALMAR.) Papa, Papa, aren't you happy at all—?

HJALMAR (*Avoiding her.*) Happy! (*Paces the floor.*) My God! Now I'm beginning to see! What vistas! What perspectives are unfolding before me! It's Hedvig; she's the one he's being so generous to!

GINA. Yes, after all, it's Hedvig who's havin' the birthday—

HEDVIG. And you'll get it anyway, Papa! You know that I'm going to give all the money to you and Mother.

HJALMAR. To your mother, yes. That's just it.

GREGERS. Hjalmar, this is a trap he's setting for you.

HJALMAR. Do you think it's another trap? Now? Again?

GREGERS. When he was here this morning he said, "Hjalmar Ekdal isn't the man you think he is."

HJALMAR. Isn't the man—!?

GREGERS. "You'll see," he said.

HJALMAR. You were supposed to see that I'd let myself be bought off—!

HEDVIG. Mother, what's this all about?

GINA. Go take off your coat.

(HEDVIG *goes out to the kitchen; she's on the verge of tears.*)

GREGERS. Yes, Hjalmar, now we'll see who's right —he or I.

HJALMAR (*Slowly tears the paper across and lays both pieces on the table.*) Here is my answer.

GREGERS. That's what I expected.

HJALMAR (*Goes to* GINA *who is standing by the stove, and says softly.*) And now, no more lies! If the relationship between you and him was completely over when you—fell in love with me, as you call it— why did he make it possible for us to get married?

GINA. I suppose he thought he'd be able to come and go as he pleased—here in our house.

HJALMAR. Is that all? Wasn't he afraid of a certain possibility?

GINA. I don't know what you mean.

HJALMAR. I want to know whether—your child has the right to live under my roof—

GINA (*Straightens up; her eyes flashing.*) And *you* ask that!

HJALMAR. You've got to answer me this one question: Does Hedvig belong to me—or? Well!

GINA (*Looking at him with cold defiance.*) I don't know.

HJALMAR (*Trembling slightly.*) You don't know!

GINA. How can *I* tell. The kind of woman I am—

HJALMAR (*Quietly, turns away from her.*) Then I'm through in this house.

GREGERS. Think what you're doing, Hjalmar!

HJALMAR (*Puts on his overcoat.*) For a man like me there's nothing to think about.

GREGERS. Yes, there's a *lot* to think of. The three of

you must be together, if you're ever going to achieve the great self-sacrifice of utter forgiveness.

HJALMAR. I don't want to achieve it. Never, never! My hat! (*Takes his hat.*) My home has come crashing down around me. (*Bursts into tears.*) Gregers, I have no child!

HEDVIG (*Who has opened the door to the kitchen.*) What are you saying? (*She runs to him.*) Papa, Papa!

GINA. Now you've done it!

HJALMAR. Don't come near me, Hedvig! Go away, far away. I can't stand seeing you. Oh, those eyes—! Good-bye.

(*He goes towards the door.*)

HEDVIG (*Hanging onto him, and screaming loudly.*) No, no! Don't go away from me!

GINA (*Shouts.*) Look at the child, Hjalmar! Look at the child!

HJALMAR. I won't! I can't! I've got to get out of here—away from all this!

(*He tears himself free from* HEDVIG *and goes out the hall door.*)

HEDVIG (*With desperation in her eyes.*) He's leaving us, Mother. He's going away from us! He'll never come back again!

GINA. Don't cry, Hedvig. Your father will be back.

HEDVIG (*Throws herself on the sofa, weeping violently.*) No, no, he'll never come back to us.

GREGERS. Do you believe that I intended it all for the best, Mrs. Ekdal?

GINA. Yes, I guess I do. But God forgive you, all the same—

HEDVIG (*Lying on the sofa.*) Oh, I'll die, I'll die! What have I done to him? Mother, you've got to get him to come home again!

GINA. Yes, yes, yes; just be quiet. I'll go out and see if I can find him. (*Puts on her coat and hat.*) Maybe he went down to Mr. Relling's. But don't lie there and bawl, you hear? Promise me?

HEDVIG (*Crying spasmodically.*) Yes, I'll stop, if Papa'll just come back!

GREGERS (*To* GINA, *as she leaves.*) Wouldn't it be better if you let him fight it out alone first?

GINA. He'll have to do that afterwards. First of all we'll have to get the child calmed down.

(*She goes out into the hall.*)

HEDVIG (*Sits up and wipes away her tears.*) Now you've got to tell me what it's all about. Why won't Papa have anything to do with me any more?

GREGERS. You shouldn't ask about that until you're a big girl—all grown up.

HEDVIG (*Hiccoughs.*) But I can't go on being unhappy like this until I'm grown up.—I bet I know what it is.—Maybe I'm not really Papa's child.

GREGERS (*Uncomfortably.*) How could that be?

HEDVIG. Maybe Mother found me. And now maybe Papa has found out. I've read about things like that.

GREGERS. Well, suppose that's what it is—

HEDVIG. I should think he could like me just as much anyway. Almost more even. After all, the wild duck was sent to us as a present, too. And I like it a lot, just the same.

GREGERS (*Changing the subject.*) Yes, that's right, the wild duck! Let's talk a little about her, Hedvig.

HEDVIG. The poor thing! He can't stand to see her either, any more. Can you imagine! He wants to wring her neck!

GREGERS. Oh, I'm sure he won't do that.

HEDVIG. No, but he said he wanted to, and I think that was an awful thing for him to say. I pray for the wild duck every night, and ask the good Lord to keep her from death and everything that is evil.

GREGERS (*Looking at her.*) You say your prayers every night?

HEDVIG. Uh-huh.

GREGERS. Who got you into that habit?

HEDVIG. I did. It was once when Papa was so sick and had boils all over his neck and the doctor had put leeches on them. He said that he was sitting there with death staring him in the face.

GREGERS. Well?

HEDVIG. So I prayed for him, when I went to bed. And since then I've kept it up.

GREGERS. And now you pray for the wild duck, too?

HEDVIG. I thought it was better to include her. She was so weak when we first got her.

GREGERS. Do you say your prayers in the morning, too?

HEDVIG. No, of course, I don't.

GREGERS. Why not then just as well?

HEDVIG. Well, you know in the morning it's light, so then there isn't really anything to be afraid of.

GREGERS. And this wild duck that you love so much, your father was going to wring her neck?

HEDVIG. No, he said it would be better for him if

he did, but he'd spare it for my sake; and that was so nice of him, don't you think?

GREGERS (*Comes a little closer to her.*) What if you voluntarily sacrificed her for his sake?

HEDVIG (*Rising.*) The wild duck!

GREGERS. Suppose you were generous enough to give up the dearest thing you have in the world?

HEDVIG. Do you think that would help?

GREGERS. Try it, Hedvig.

HEDVIG (*Softly, with shining eyes.*) All right, I will.

GREGERS. Can you go through with it?

HEDVIG. I'll ask Grandpa to shoot her for me.

GREGERS. Yes, do that. But don't say a word to your mother about it.

HEDVIG. Why not?

GREGERS. She doesn't understand us.

HEDVIG. The wild duck? I'm going to try it tomorrow morning.

(GINA *comes in from the hall.*)

HEDVIG (*Going to meet her.*) Did you find him, mother?

GINA. No, but I heard he'd stopped by and picked up Mr. Relling.

GREGERS. Are you sure?

GINA. That's what the janitor's wife said. Molvik went along too, she said.

GREGERS. And that at a time when his mind needs so badly to fight it out in solitude—!

GINA (*Taking off her coat and hat.*) Yes, men are funny, that's what they are. God only knows where Mr. Relling has taken him to . . . I ran over to Mrs. Eriksen's, but they wasn't there.

HEDVIG (*Fighting back her tears.*) What if he never comes home again!

GREGERS. He's *coming* home. I'll go and see him first thing in the morning and *then* you'll see *how* he comes. You just put your faith in that, and sleep well, Hedvig. Good night.

(*He goes out into the hall.*)

HEDVIG (*Throws herself into* GINA's *arms, weeping violently.*) Mama, Mama!

GINA (*Pats her back, and sighs.*) Oh yes, Mr. Relling was right, that's a fact. This is what happens when crazy fools come around—shovin' their fine ideas at you—their complicated claims of—somethin'-or-other—

Act Five

❧

THE SCENE: (*Hjalmar Ekdal's studio. The cold, grey light of morning. Wet snow on the large panes of the skylight.*

AT RISE: GINA *comes in from the kitchen, carrying a feather duster and a dust cloth. She is wearing a kitchen apron. Crosses toward the door to the living room. Before she reaches it,* HEDVIG *comes in hurriedly from the hall.*)

GINA (*Stops.*) Well?

HEDVIG. Yes, Mother, I'm pretty sure he's down at Mr. Relling's—

GINA. There, you see!

HEDVIG. The janitor's wife said she heard Mr. Relling brought two people home with him last night.

GINA. That's just what I thought.

HEDVIG. But what's the use when he won't come up to us?

GINA. At least I can go down and talk to him.

(OLD EKDAL *appears in the doorway to his room. He's wearing his robe and slippers, and smoking his pipe.*)

EKDAL. Say, Hjalmar—. Isn't Hjalmar home?

GINA. No, I guess he's gone out.

EKDAL. So early? In such a blizzard? Well, well, never mind. I can take my morning walk alone. Yessir.

116

(*He opens the sliding door to the attic.* HEDVIG
*helps him; he goes in; she closes the door be-
hind him.*)

HEDVIG (*Softly.*) Oh, Mother, when poor Grandpa
hears that Papa wants to leave us, what then?

GINA. Oh, bah! Grandpa mustn't hear anything
about it. It was lucky he wasn't home yesterday during all that hullabaloo.

HEDVIG. Yes, but—

(GREGERS *comes in from the hall.*)

GREGERS. Well, have you picked up his trail?

GINA. He seems to be down at Mr. Relling's.

GREGERS. Relling! You mean he's really been out
with those people?

GINA. I guess he has.

GREGERS. Just when he needed to be alone, to pull
himself together, seriously—

GINA. That's the truth.

(RELLING *comes in from the hall.*)

HEDVIG (*Going towards him.*) Is Papa in your
room?

GINA (*At the same time.*) Is he there?

RELLING. He certainly is.

HEDVIG. And you didn't come and tell us!

RELLING. No, I'm a monster. But first I had to calm
down the other monster; I mean our little demon
naturally; and then I fell so fast asleep that—

GINA. What does Hjalmar say today?

RELLING. Not a thing in the world.

HEDVIG. Doesn't he say anything?

RELLING. Not a blessed word.

GREGERS. No, of course; I can understand that.

GINA. But what's he doin'?

RELLING. He's lying on the sofa, snoring.

GINA. Oh? Yes, Hjalmar can really snore.

HEDVIG. He's sleeping? Can he sleep?

RELLING. Sure as hell looks that way.

GREGERS. That's understandable; after the struggle that's been raging in him—

GINA. And he isn't used to being out nights.

HEDVIG. Maybe it's just as well he's getting some sleep, Mother.

GINA. I think so, too; but then we'd better not stir him up too early. Thank you, Mr. Relling. Now then —first, I'll fix the house up a little and then—come and help me, Hedvig.

(GINA *and* HEDVIG *go into the living room.*)

GREGERS (*Turning to* RELLING.) Tell me about the spiritual struggle that's taking place in Hjalmar Ekdal?

RELLING. My God, I haven't noticed that there's any "spiritual struggle" in him.

GREGERS. What? At such a turning point? When his whole life has gotten a new foundation—? How can you think that a man of Hjalmar's character—?

RELLING. Character! Him? If he ever had any leaning towards the sort of abnormality you call "character" it was thoroughly extirpated, root and branch, while he was still a boy. That I can assure you.

GREGERS. That would be very strange,—considering all the love he enjoyed while he was being brought up.

RELLING. By those two frustrated, hysterical, spinster aunts, you mean?

GREGERS. I'll tell you one thing: they were women who never forgot the claim of the ideal— Well, I suppose you'll start sneering again.

RELLING. No, I'm not in the mood for that. Anyway, I know all about it. He's vomited up all sorts of rhetoric about those "twin soul-mothers" of his. But I don't think he's got much to thank them for. Hjalmar's misfortune is that among his friends he's always been regarded as a shining light—

GREGERS. Well, isn't he? I mean, look at the depth of his mind!

RELLING. *I've* never noticed it. That his father thought so—well, let that pass. After all, the old lieutenant's been a fool all his life.

GREGERS. All his life he's been a man with the heart of a child; that's what you don't understand.

RELLING. All right. But then, when our dear, sweet Hjalmar had gotten into college some way or other,— right away he was the great shining light of the future among his classmates, too. Oh, he was pretty, all right, the big lout. Pink and white—just the way the little schoolgirls like their fellows; and since he was so easily moved emotionally, and had this heart-rending voice, and since he was so clever at declaiming other people's verses and other people's thoughts—

GREGERS (*Angrily.*) Are you talking about Hjalmar Ekdal?

RELLING. Yes, do you mind? That's the way he looks inside, this idol you're flat on your belly in front of.

GREGERS. I don't think I am that completely blind.

RELLING. Oh yes, not far from it. You're a sick man, too, you see.

GREGERS. You're right there.

RELLING. Uh-huh. You're a very complicated case. First of all, there's this horrible feverish righteousness, and then—what's even worse—you're always wallowing in a delirium of hero worship. You've always got to have something to admire, something beyond your reach.

GREGERS. Yes, it's true I have to look for it outside myself.

RELLING. But you've been mistaken about every single marvellous—louse, you think you've discovered. This time, too, you've come to a poor homestead with your claim of the ideal; and again there's no cash on hand.

GREGERS. If you don't think any better of Hjalmar Ekdal than that, how can you get any pleasure out of being with him all the time.

RELLING. My God! I'm ashamed to remind you, but I'm supposed to be some sort of a doctor. So I've got to take care of the poor sick people who live in the same house with me.

GREGERS. I see! Hjalmar Ekdal is sick, too?

RELLING. Nearly everybody is, I'm sorry to say.

GREGERS. And how are you trying to cure him?

RELLING. My usual way. I see to it that the life lie, the illusion, is kept alive in him.

GREGERS. The life lie? I didn't quite get that—?

RELLING. That's what I said, the life lie. Because that's the narcotic, you see.

GREGERS. May I ask what kind of a lie Hjalmar is addicted to?

RELLING. No, thank you; I don't betray my secrets to quacks. You'd be quite capable of messing him up even worse for me. But the method is tested and sound. I have used it on Molvik, too. I made him "daemonic." That's the way I had to drain his poison off.

GREGERS. Then he isn't daemonic?

RELLING. What the devil does that mean—to be daemonic? That's just some nonsense I invented to save what little life he had left in him. If I hadn't, the poor good-natured pig would have folded up in self-contempt and despair a hell of a long time ago. And then there's the old lieutenant! But of course, he's hit on his own cure.

GREGERS. Lt. Ekdal? What about him?

RELLING. Well, what do you think? The bear-hunter, in there in the attic shooting rabbits? There isn't a happier sportsman in the world than he when he's allowed to play around in there among all the old junk. Those four or five dried-up Xmas trees he's been hoarding in there, to him they're the same thing as the huge, fresh Highdale forest. The rooster and all the chickens, they're the game birds swaying high in the pine trees; and the rabbits going humpety-bump along the attic floor, they're the black bears that he tackles—the mighty hero of the great outdoors!

GREGERS. That miserable old man! He's certainly had to mark down the ideals of his youth.

RELLING. While I think of it, Mr. Werle, Junior—don't use that foreign word: "ideals." We have a good Norwegian word for it: "lies."

GREGERS. Do you mean those two things are related to each other?

RELLING. Yes, about like typhus and gangrene.

GREGERS. Dr. Relling, I'm not going to give in until I've rescued Hjalmar from your claws!

RELLING. The worse for *him*. If you take the life

lie away from the average man, you rob him of happiness at the same time. (*To* HEDVIG, *who comes in from the living room.*) Well, little mother of the wild duck, I'm going to see if your old man's still lying there pondering that remarkable invention of his.

(*He goes out into the hall.*)

GREGERS (*Goes close to* HEDVIG.) I can see that you haven't done it yet.

HEDVIG. What? Oh, the wild duck! No.

GREGERS. I suppose you didn't have the nerve when the time came to do something about it—

HEDVIG. No, it isn't that. But when I woke up this morning and remembered what we'd been talking about I thought it was so funny.

GREGERS. Funny?

HEDVIG. Well, I don't know—. Last night, right at the moment I thought that there was something wonderful to it; but after I'd slept and then thought of it again, it didn't seem like it would help much.

GREGERS. No, I don't suppose you've grown up here without having lost something of yourself.

HEDVIG. I don't care about that. If Papa would just come up—

GREGERS. Oh, if you just had eyes for the things that give life value—if you just had a really generous heart, you'd see how he'd come up to you! But I still believe in you, Hedvig. Yes, I do.

(*He goes out into the hall.* HEDVIG *wanders around the room. Then she starts for the kitchen. There is a knock at the attic door. She goes and opens it slightly.* OLD EKDAL *comes in; she closes the door behind him.*)

EKDAL. Hmm, it's not much fun to take your morning walk alone, my girl.

HEDVIG. Wouldn't you like to go hunting, Grandpa?

EKDAL. It's no kind of weather for hunting today. It's so dark you can't see your hand in front of your face.

HEDVIG. Don't you ever want to shoot anything but rabbits?

EKDAL. Aren't the rabbits good enough?

HEDVIG. How about the wild duck?

EKDAL (*Chuckles a little.*) Are you scared I'm going to shoot your duck, huh? Not a chance, my girl. Not a chance.

HEDVIG. No, I suppose you couldn't. I guess it's very difficult to shoot ducks.

EKDAL. Couldn't!? I guess I could, all right.

HEDVIG. How would you do it, Grandpa?—I don't mean with my wild duck, but with other ones?

EKDAL. I'd see to it I got 'em right in the breast, you understand! That's the surest way. And you have to shoot against the feathers, you see—not with the feathers.

HEDVIG. Do they die then, Grandpa?

EKDAL. Die? Hell, yes—if you shoot right. Well, I'd better go in and clean up a little. Hmm—you understand—hmm.

(*He goes into his room.* HEDVIG *waits a moment, glances towards the living room door, goes to the bookcase, stands on tiptoe, gets the double-bar-*

*relled pistol down from the shelf and looks at it.
GINA comes in from the living room carrying her
whisk broom and dust cloth. HEDVIG quickly puts
the pistol back, unnoticed.*)

GINA. Don't play with your father's things, Hedvig.
HEDVIG (*Goes away from the bookcase.*) I just
wanted to straighten them out a little.
GINA. You'd better go out in the kitchen, and see
if the coffee's still warm. I want to take him a tray
when I go down to him.

(HEDVIG *goes out.* GINA *begins to sweep and
clean the studio. After a moment, the hall door
is opened hesitantly, and* HJALMAR EKDAL *looks
in. He has his overcoat on, but has no hat. He
is unwashed, and his hair is unkempt. His eyes
are bleary and dull.*)

GINA (*Remains standing with the broom in her
hand and looks at him.*) Why, Hjalmar—so you came
back after all?
HJALMAR. (*Comes in and speaks dully.*) I've come
—only to leave again right away.
GINA. Yes, yes, of course, I know. My good gracious,
the way you look!
HJALMAR. Look?
GINA. And your lovely winter coat! It's certainly
gotten a going over.
HEDVIG (*At the kitchen door.*) Mother, don't you
want me to—? (*She sees* HJALMAR, *cries out with
happiness, and runs towards him.*) Papa, Papa!
HJALMAR (*Turns away, and makes a gesture of re-*

pulsion.) Get away! Get away! (*To* GINA.) Get her away from me, I tell you!

GINA (*Softly.*) Go into the living room, Hedvig.

(HEDVIG *leaves silently.*)

HJALMAR (*Busily opens the table drawer.*) I've got to have my books with me. Where are my books?

GINA. Which books?

HJALMAR. My scientific library, of course; the technical periodicals I use for my invention.

GINA (*Looking through the bookcase.*) You mean those paper-covered ones?

HJALMAR. Of course.

GINA (*Puts a pile of pamphlets on the table.*) Don't you want me to get Hedvig to cut the pages for you?

HJALMAR. Nobody needs to cut anything for me.

(*A short silence.*)

GINA. You're still set on leaving us, Hjalmar?

HJALMAR (*Rummaging among the books.*) Yes, that's obvious, I should think.

GINA. All right, all right.

HJALMAR (*Violently.*) How can I stay here and have the knife twisted in me every hour of the day!

GINA. God forgive you! How can you think such an awful thing about me?

HJALMAR. Give me proof—!

GINA. I think you're the one that ought to give proof.

HJALMAR. After a past like yours? There are certain demands—I'm tempted to call them the very claims of the ideal—

GINA. But what about the old man? What's goin' to become of him?—the poor old fellow?

HJALMAR. I know my duty; I'll take the poor, help-less, old man with me. I'm going out to make arrange-ments—Hmm— (*Hesitantly.*) Hasn't anybody found my hat on the stairs?

GINA. No. Have you lost your hat?

HJALMAR. Naturally I was wearing it when I came home last night; there's no doubt about that; but I couldn't find it this morning.

GINA. My God! Where did you go with them two drunkards?

HJALMAR. Oh, don't bother me with such trivial matters. Do you think I'm in the mood to remember details?

GINA. I hope you haven't caught cold, Hjalmar—

(*She goes out in the kitchen.*)

HJALMAR (*Talks to himself in a low angry voice, as he empties the table drawer.*) You're a scoundrel, Relling!—A villain, that's what you are! Leading a man to—!—I wish I could get somebody to put a knife in you.

(*He puts some old letters aside, finds the torn document from the day before, picks it up, and looks at the pieces. He puts it down quickly as* GINA *comes in.*)

GINA (*Puts a tray with breakfast things on the table.*) Here's a drop of somethin' hot in case you want it. And some bread and butter and a few cold cuts.

HJALMAR (*Glances at the tray.*) Cold cuts? Not under this roof! Of course, I haven't had solid food in almost twenty-four hours; but never mind about that.—My notes! The beginning of my memoirs! Where is my diary—and my important papers? (*He opens the door to the living room, but steps back.*) She's here, too!

GINA. Well, good heavens, the child's got to be some place!

HJALMAR. Get out.

(HJALMAR *steps aside, and* HEDVIG *comes into the studio, frightened.*)

HJALMAR (*With his hand on the doorknob, to* GINA.) During the last moments I spend in my former house, I wish to be spared the presence of intruders—

(*Goes into the living room.*)

HEDVIG (*With a sudden rush towards her mother, asks softly, trembling.*) Is that me?

GINA. Stay in the kitchen, Hedvig; or, no—you'd better go into your own room. (*Speaks to* HJALMAR *as she goes into the living room.*) Wait a minute, Hjalmar; don't mess around in the drawers like that. *I* know where everything is.

HEDVIG (*Frightened and bewildered, stands motionless for a moment. She is biting her lips to keep back the tears. She clenches her hands convulsively, and says softly*): The wild duck!

(*She steals over and takes the pistol from the shelf, opens the door to the attic a little way,*

slips in, and closes the door after her. HJALMAR
and GINA *begin to argue in the livingroom.*)

HJALMAR (*Appears with some notebooks and old
loose papers, which he puts on the table.*) Oh, what
good is that bag? There'll be a thousand things I'll
have to drag with me.

GINA (*Follows with the suitcases.*) Well, then,
leave all the other things for a while, and just take
a shirt and a pair of woolen drawers with you.

HJALMAR. Whew! These exhausting preparations!

(*He takes his overcoat off and throws it on the
sofa.*)

GINA. And the coffee's standin' there gettin' cold.

HJALMAR. Hmm. (*Automatically drinks a mouth-
ful, and then another one.*)

GINA (*Dusting the back of the chairs.*) The hard-
est thing for you will be to find another big attic for
the rabbits.

HJALMAR. What! Am I supposed to drag all those
rabbits with me, too?

GINA. Well, I'm sure the old man can't get along
without his rabbits.

HJALMAR. He'll just have to get used to it. I'm giving up more important things than rabbits!

GINA (*Dusting the bookcase.*) Do you want me to
put your flute in the bag?

HJALMAR. No. No flute for me. But give me the
pistol!

GINA. You goin' to take that pigstol with you?

HJALMAR. Yes, my loaded pistol.

GINA (*Looking for it.*) It's gone. He must have taken it in there with him.

HJALMAR. Is he in the attic?

GINA. Sure he's in there.

HJALMAR. Hmm—poor, lonely, old fellow.

(*He picks up a piece of bread and butter, eats it, and drains his cup of coffee.*)

GINA. If we hadn't rented the room, you could have moved in there.

HJALMAR. I should stay under the same roof with—! Never—*never!*

GINA. But couldn't you just stay in the living room —just for a day or two? You'd have everything to yourself there.

HJALMAR. Not within these walls!

GINA. Well, down with Relling and Molvik then.

HJALMAR. Don't mention their names to me! Just the thought of them is enough to make me lose my appetite.—Oh no, I guess I'll have to go out into the howling blizzard—go from house to house, looking for shelter for my father and myself.

GINA. But you haven't got a hat, Hjalmar! You've lost your hat.

HJALMAR. Oh, those two scoundrels—filled with perversion! I'll have to get hold of a hat. (*Takes another piece of bread and butter.*) I've got to do something about it. I've no intention of sacrificing my life.

(*Looks for something on the tray.*)

GINA. What are you lookin' for?

HJALMAR. Butter.

GINA. I'll get some right away.

(*She goes to the kitchen.*)

HJALMAR (*Calls after her.*) Oh, don't bother. Dry bread is good enough for me.

GINA (*Brings in a butter dish.*) Here; it's supposed to be fresh.

(*She pours another cup of coffee for him; he sits on the sofa, adds more butter to the bread, eats, and drinks for a while in silence.*)

HJALMAR. Could I—without having somebody hanging over me all the time—nobody, you understand—could I stay in the living room for a day or two?

GINA. Of course you could, if you only would.

HJALMAR. Because I can't see any possibility of getting all of Father's things out on such short notice.

GINA. And then there's this, too: you've gotta tell him that you don't want to live with us no more.

HJALMAR (*Shoves the coffee cup away.*) Yes, that, too. I'm going to be forced to untangle this whole mess again—I've got to think. I've got to have a little time. I can't shoulder all the burdens in one day.

GINA. No, 'specially not when it's such bad weather.

HJALMAR (*Moves* MR. WERLE's *letter around a little.*) I see that paper's still lying around here.

GINA. *I* haven't touched it.

HJALMAR. Of course, it's none of my business—

GINA. Well, *I* don't intend to make use of it.

HJALMAR. It would be too bad if it disappeared

altogether; in all the commotion when I'm moving, it might easily be—

GINA. I'll take care of it, Hjalmar.

HJALMAR. After all, the deed of gift belongs to Father first off, and it'll have to be his affair whether he uses it or not.

GINA (*Sighs.*) Yes, poor old Dad—

HJALMAR. Just for safety's sake—. Where's some paste?

GINA (*Goes to the bookcase.*) Here's the pot.

HJALMAR. And a brush.

GINA. Here's a brush, too.

(*She brings him the things.*)

HJALMAR (*Taking a pair of scissors.*) Just a strip of paper on the back— (*Clips and glues.*) Far be it from me to lay a hand on someone else's property— and least of all on a poverty-stricken old man's—and on—well, the other one's either. There now. Let it lie there for a while, and as soon as it's dry, take it away. I don't want to see this document again. Ever!

(GREGERS WERLE *comes in from the hall.*)

GREGERS (*Somewhat surprised.*) What—are you sitting here, Hjalmar?

HJALMAR (*Standing quickly.*) I just dropped down with weariness.

GREGERS. You've eaten lunch though, I see.

HJALMAR. The body makes its claims once in a while, too.

GREGERS. What have you decided?

HJALMAR. For a man like me there is only one path to take. I'm in the process of gathering together my most important possessions. But it takes time, naturally.

GINA (*A little impatient.*) Well, am I supposed to fix the living room for you, or pack the suitcase?

HJALMAR (*With a glance of irritation at* GREGERS.) Pack—and fix the room!

GINA (*Taking the suitcase.*) All right, then. I'll pack the shirt and the other things.

(*She goes into the living room and closes the door behind her.*)

GREGERS (*After a short silence.*) I never thought that this would be the end of it. Is it really necessary for you to leave your home?

HJALMAR (*Walks restlessly about the room.*) What do you want me to do?—I'm not made for unhappiness, Gregers. It's essential for me to be in a comfortable and peaceful and secure environment.

GREGERS. But can't you be? Why don't you try? It looks to me as if you have solid ground to build on now—so why don't you start again? And remember, you have your invention to live for.

HJALMAR. Agh, don't talk about that invention. That may be *very* far off.

GREGERS. Oh?

HJALMAR. Yes, my God, what is it actually you want me to invent? Almost everything is invented already—by others. It gets harder every day—

GREGERS. But you've put such a lot of work into this.

HJALMAR. It was that—that dissolute Relling who got me to do it.

GREGERS. Relling?

HJALMAR. Yes, he was the one who first pointed out my aptitude for making some unusual photographic invention.

GREGERS. I see—it was Relling!

HJALMAR. Oh, it used to make me so happy! Not so much for the sake of the invention itself, but because Hedvig believed in it—believed in it with all the strength of a child's heart.—That is, I've been fool enough to think she had faith in it.

GREGERS. Do you really think that Hedvig could be false to you?

HJALMAR. It doesn't matter what I think now. It's Hedvig who's standing in my way. She's shutting the sun out of my whole life.

GREGERS. Hedvig! Are you talking about Hedvig? How can *she* shut anything out of your life?

HJALMAR (*Without answering.*) You've no idea how I have loved that child! You've no idea how happy I was every time I came home to this poor room, and she flew to meet me, with her sweet, blinking eyes. Oh, I'm a trusting fool! I loved her so much —so I created the beautiful dream that she loved me, too.

GREGERS. Do you think that was only a dream?

HJALMAR. How do I know? I can't force Gina to tell me anything; and besides she lacks completely all feeling about the ideal side of these complications. But to you I feel I must open my heart, Gregers. There's this horrible doubt—perhaps Hedvig has never really, honestly loved me.

GREGERS. Maybe you could get proof of that. (*He listens.*) What's that? I think I hear the wild duck crying—?

HJALMAR. Yes, it *is* quacking. My father's in the attic.

GREGERS. Is he? (*His face lights with pleasure.*) As I was saying, perhaps you might get proof that poor, little Hedvig loves you!

HJALMAR. Ah, what proof can she give me? I'm afraid to believe in any assurance from that direction.

GREGERS. I'm certain Hedvig doesn't know what deceit means.

HJALMAR. Oh Gregers, that's exactly what's not so certain. Who knows what Gina and this Mrs. Sörby may have sat here lots of times and whispered and gossiped about? Hedvig usually keeps her ears open. Perhaps that deed of gift wasn't such a surprise to her after all. I thought I felt something like that.

GREGERS. What's gotten into you?

HJALMAR. My eyes have been opened. You just wait; you'll see: that deed of gift is only the beginning. Mrs. Sörby has always had a soft spot for Hedvig; and now she's got the power to do whatever she pleases for the child. They can take her away from me any time they feel like it.

GREGERS. Hedvig would never in this world leave *you!*

HJALMAR. Don't be so sure of that. What if they offer her everything in the world—? Oh, I've loved her so unspeakably! It would have been my greatest happiness to take her gently by the hand and lead her, as you'd lead a child afraid of the dark through a great deserted room!—I am absolutely certain now that the poor photographer in the garret has never really been anything to her. It's just that she's been shrewd enough to stay on good terms with him till the time came.

GREGERS. You don't believe this yourself, Hjalmar!

HJALMAR. That's just what's so terrible—I don't know what to believe—I'll never know. But do you really doubt that it must be this way? (*He laughs.*) You have too much faith in the claim of the ideal, my good Gregers! If the others were to come, with bulging pockets, and call to the child: "Leave him; we'll give you *life*—!"

GREGERS (*Quickly.*) Well, what do you think would happen then?

HJALMAR. Suppose I were to ask her then: "Hedvig, are you willing to give up life for me?" (*He laughs contemptuously.*) No, thank you! You'd hear what kind of an answer I'd get.

(*A shot is heard in the attic.*)

GREGERS (*Cries out in happiness.*) Hjalmar!

HJALMAR. Oh God, he has to chose right now to go hunting!

GINA (*Comes in.*) Ugh, Hjalmar, I think the old man is in the attic blazin' away all by himself.

HJALMAR. I'll take a look—

GREGERS (*Eagerly, moved.*) Wait a minute! Do you know what that was?

HJALMAR. Of course, I know.

GREGERS. No you don't. But *I* do. That was the proof!

HJALMAR. What proof?

GREGERS. It was an innocent sacrifice. She's gotten your father to shoot the wild duck.

HJALMAR. Shoot the wild duck!

GINA. Why, what in the—!

HJALMAR. What good is that supposed to do?

GREGERS. She wanted to sacrifice her dearest possession for you. She thought that then you'd be bound to love her again.

HJALMAR (*Softly, moved.*) Oh, that child!

GINA. What things she can think of.

GREGERS. She just wanted to have your love back, Hjalmar. She didn't see how she could live without it.

GINA (*Fighting back her tears.*) There you see for yourself, Hjalmar.

HJALMAR. Gina, where is she?

GINA (*Sniffing.*) The poor thing, I suppose she's sittin' out in the kitchen.

HJALMAR (*Goes and tears open the kitchen door.*) Hedvig, come here! Come in here to me! (*He looks around.*) No, she's not here.

GINA. Maybe she's in her room then.

HJALMAR (*Outside.*) She isn't here either. (*Comes back in.*) She must have gone out.

GINA. Well, you didn't want her any place in the house.

HJALMAR. Oh, if she'd just come home, so I can really tell her—. Everything's going to be all right now, Gregers. I think that now we can start life all over again.

GREGERS (*Quietly.*) I knew it; I knew that redemption would come through the child.

(OLD EKDAL *appears in the door to his room. He is in full uniform, and is busy buckling his sword belt around his waist.*)

HJALMAR (*Astounded.*) Father! Were you in there?

GINA. Were you shootin' in your room, Grandpa?

EKDAL (*Coming closer; angrily.*) So you go hunting all by yourself do you, Hjalmar?

HJALMAR (*Tensely, bewildered.*) It wasn't you shooting in the attic?

EKDAL. Who, me, shooting? Hmm.

GREGERS (*Crying out to* HJALMAR.) Hjalmar, she has shot the wild duck herself!

HJALMAR. What *is* this? (*He runs to the attic door, tears it open, looks in, and cries out.*) Hedvig!

GINA (*Running to the door.*) Good God, what is it!

HJALMAR (*Goes into the attic.*) She's lying on the floor!

GREGERS. Hedvig! Lying on the floor!

(*He goes in to* HJALMAR.)

GINA (*Simultaneously.*) Hedvig! (*She disappears into the attic.*) No, no, no!

EKDAL (*With a chuckle.*) Is she going hunting too, now?

(HJALMAR, GINA, *and* GREGERS *carry* HEDVIG *into the studio; the pistol is clenched in her dangling right hand.*)

HJALMAR (*Almost out of his mind.*) The pistol went off. She hit herself. Call for help! Help!

GINA (*Runs out into the hall; and shouts down the stairs.*) Relling! Relling! Doctor Relling! Come up here! Hurry, hurry!

(HJALMAR *and* GREGERS *place* HEDVIG *on the sofa.*)

EKDAL (*Quietly.*) The woods avenge.

HJALMAR (*Kneeling by* HEDVIG.) She'll come to in a minute. She'll come to—. Yes, yes, yes.

GINA (*Who has returned.*) Where has she hit herself? I can't see anything—

(RELLING *comes in quickly; he is followed almost immediately by* MOLVIK *wearing the coat of his dress suit, without vest or necktie.*)

RELLING. What's the matter?

GINA. They're sayin' that Hedvig has shot herself.

HJALMAR. Come and help us!

RELLING. Shot herself!

(*He moves the table aside and begins to examine her.*)

HJALMAR (*Still kneeling, looks up at him in fear.*) It can't be dangerous? Can it, Relling? She's hardly bleeding at all. It can't be dangerous?

RELLING. How did it happen?

HJALMAR. Oh, how do I know—

GINA. She wanted to shoot the wild duck.

RELLING. The wild duck?

HJALMAR. The pistol must have gone off.

RELLING. Hmm. I see.

EKDAL. The woods avenge! But I'm not afraid, anyway.

(*He goes into the attic and closes the door.*)

HJALMAR. Well, Relling, why don't you say something?

RELLING. The bullet has entered the breast.

HJALMAR. Yes, but she'll be all right, won't she?

RELLING. You can see that Hedvig is dead, can't you?

GINA (*Bursts into tears.*) Oh, my child, my child—

GREGERS (*Hoarsely.*) In the depths of the sea—

HJALMAR (*Leaping up.*) No, no, she's got to live! Oh, please, for God's sake, Relling, just for a minute— just long enough for me to tell her how much I loved her all the time!

RELLING. It went through the heart. Internal hemorrhage. She died on the spot.

HJALMAR. And I chased her away from me like an animal! And she crept into the attic, terrified, and died for love of me! (*Sobbing.*) I can't ever make it up to her! I can't ever tell her—! (*Clenches his fists and lifts his head, crying:*) You up there—! If you really *are!* Why did you do this to me?

GINA. Shhh, shhh, you mustn't carry on so. I guess we had no right to keep her.

MOLVIK. The child is not dead, but sleepeth.

RELLING. Rot.

HJALMAR (*Quiets down, goes to the sofa, stands with folded arms, looking down at* HEDVIG.) There she lies, stiff and still.

RELLING (*Tries to wrest the pistol from her hand.*) She's holding on so tight, so tight.

GINA. No, Relling, no, don't break her fingers; let her keep the pigstol.

HJALMAR. She can take it with her.

GINA. Yes, let her. But the child mustn't lie out here for everyone to stare at. She goin' into her own little room, that's what she is. Help me, Hjalmar.

(HJALMAR *and* GINA *lift* HEDVIG *between them.*)

HJALMAR (*As they carry her out.*) Oh Gina, Gina, can you bear this!

GINA. We'll have to help each other. Because *now* I know she belongs to both of us.

MOLVIK (*Stretches his arms and mumbles.*) Blessed be the name of the Lord; dust to dust; dust to dust—

RELLING (*Whispers.*) Shut up, man! You're drunk!

(HJALMAR *and* GINA *carry the body out through the kitchen door.* RELLING *closes the door behind them.* MOLVIK *slinks out into the hall.*)

RELLING (*Goes to* GREGERS.) Nobody will ever get me to believe that this was an accident.

GREGERS (*Who has been standing terrified, with convulsive twitchings.*) Nobody can say how the terrible thing happened.

RELLING. She's got powder burns on her dress. She must have pressed the pistol right against her breast and pulled the trigger.

GREGERS. Hedvig didn't die in vain. Did you see how grief released the nobility in him?

RELLING. Nearly everyone is noble when he's confronted with death. How long do you think that nobility will last with him?

GREGERS. Why shouldn't it last, and grow, all his life?

RELLING. Before a year is up, little Hedvig will be nothing to him but a pretty subject for declamation. SPEECH

GREGERS. And you dare say that about Hjalmar Ekdal?

RELLING. We'll talk about this again, when the first

grass is withered on her grave. Then you'll hear him vomit up something about: "The child torn too early from her father's heart." And you'll see him drown himself in sentiment and self-admiration and self-pity. You wait and see!

GREGERS. If you're right and I'm wrong, life isn't worth living.

RELLING. Oh life might not be so bad at that. If we could just be left in peace by these blessed bill collectors that come running to the doors of poor people like us—with the "claim of the ideal."

GREGERS (*Looking straight before him.*) In that case, I'm glad my fate is what it is.

RELLING. If you don't mind—what is your fate?

GREGERS (*As he leaves.*) To be the thirteenth at the table.

CHRIST

RELLING. The hell you say!

SELECTED BIBLIOGRAPHY

SELECTED BIBLIOGRAPHY

The following bibliography is far from complete but contains most of the items of particular interest on Ibsen in the major languages. "Particular interest" does not necessarily mean either that one must agree with the author, or, though of a different opinion, respect his judgment. But the student will find in these books, some of which are outstanding, ideas and insights to stimulate his own—whether by concord or discord hardly matters.

Bentley, Eric, *In Search of Theater* (New York, 1953).

———, *The Life of the Drama* (New York, 1964).

———, *The Playwright as Thinker* (New York, 1946).

Bradbrook, M. C., *Ibsen, the Norwegian: A Revaluation* (London, 1947).

Brustein, Robert, *The Theatre of Revolt* (Boston, 1964).

Dobrée, Bonamy, *The Lamp and the Lute* (Oxford, 1929).

Downs, Brian W., *Ibsen, The Intellectual Background* (Cambridge, England, 1946).

———, *A Study of Six Plays by Ibsen* (Cambridge, England, 1950).

Flores, Angel, ed., *Ibsen: A Marxist Analysis* (New York, 1937).

Forster, E. M., *Abinger Harvest* (London, 1953).

Hofmannsthal, Hugo v., *Prosa I* (Frankfurt a. M., 1950).

Ibsen, Henrik, *Letters and Speeches*, ed. by Evert Sprinchorn (New York, 1964).

Jacobs, Monty, *Ibsen's Bühnentechnik* (Dresden, 1920).

James, Henry, *The Scenic Art*, ed. by Allen Wade (New York, 1957).

Jorgenson, T., *Henrik Ibsen, A Study in Art and Personality* (Northfield, Minn., 1945).

Knight, G. Wilson, *Henrik Ibsen* (Edinburgh, 1962).

Koht, Halvdan, *The Life of Ibsen* (New York, 1931).

Logeman, Henri, *A Commentary on Henrik Ibsen's Peer Gynt: Its Language, Literary Associations and Folklore* (The Hague, 1917).

Lucas, F. L., *The Drama of Ibsen and Strindberg* (London and New York, 1962).

McFarlane, James W., *Ibsen and the Temper of Norwegian Literature* (London, 1960).

Mohr, Otto Lous, *Henrik Ibsen som Maler: With an English Summary* (Oslo, 1953).

Northam, John, *Ibsen's Dramatic Method* (London, 1953).

Peacock, Ronald, *The Poet in the Theatre* (London, 1946).

Shaw, George Bernard, *The Quintessence of Ibsenism* (London, 1891).

Suarès, André, *Trois Hommes* (Paris, 1935).

Szondi, Peter, *Theorie des modernen Dramas* (Frankfurt a. M., 1956).

Tennant, P. F. D., *Ibsen's Dramatic Technique* (London, 1948).

Valency, Maurice, *The Flower and the Castle* (New York, 1963).

Weigand, Hermann J., *The Modern Ibsen* (New York, 1925).

Williams, Raymond, *Drama from Ibsen to Eliot* (London, 1952).

Zucker, A. E., *Ibsen, the Master Builder* (New York, 1929).